Fine Feathers

A Quilter's Guide to Customizing Traditional Feather Quilting Designs

by
Marianne Fons

To my husband, John, and our daughters, Hannah,
Mary Katherine and Rebecca, who still love quilts,
and to my friend, Liz Porter.

C&T Publishing, P.O. Box 1456, Lafayette, CA 94549

ACKNOWLEDGEMENTS

Special thanks to:
  Hundreds of feathering students, who eagerly embraced feathering techniques and asked for a comprehensive text;
  Liz Porter, who encouraged me to go ahead with the feathering book after her new job made her unable to participate;
  Tom and Carolie Hensley, for their interest and investment in my book, and
  Pat Wilens, my editor, for the intelligence and skill she brings to every project.

I would also like to thank Julie Silber, Barbara Brackman, Sharon Risedorph, Barb Corsbie, Luella Fairholm, Lois Wilson, Joan Van Vleet, Kent Clawson, Marilyn Lane and Joyce Gross. Finally, I appreciate the help of my husband, John Fons, with black and white photos, and of his father, Lloyd Fons, who took 72 slides of me to get an author photo, after the original picture Sharon made was lost in the mail.

© 1988 by Marianne Fons

Edited and Designed by Patricia Wilens

Illustrations by Ann Davis Nunemacher

Photos by Sharon Risedorph unless credited otherwise

Published by C&T Publishing
P.O. Box 1456, Lafayette, CA 94549

ISBN 0-914881-10-8

Library of Congress Catalog Card No.: 87-71885

Printed in the United States of America

TABLE OF CONTENTS

Introduction

The beautiful feathered quilting designs admired on classic Amish and other antique quilts are the creme de la creme of quilting. Finely-stitched feather patterns often seem the perfect echo for curved applique motifs, or the appropriate complement for hard-edged patchwork. The whole-cloth quilt, often a quilter's master work, is at its best when covered with feather fancies and scrolls, set off by a background grid.

Before I learned to create my own feather designs, I used to search for a commercial template or printed pattern of just the right size feather circle or border for my projects. Usually, my search was not perfectly successful, but it never occurred to me to draw my own feather patterns. In truth, I was intimidated by those graceful, undulating plumes from the past. I figured you had to be born Amish to originate feather designs.

Becoming an author and designer forced me to experiment with feathering. When Liz Porter and I were working on **Classic Quilted Vests*** and **Classic Basket Patterns***, we wanted to include feather quilting on some of our projects. We struggled through those first few designs and then began a study of feather quilting, which included taking plumed borders apart and putting them back together again, turning feather circles inside-out, and going to quilt shows in search of classic feathering examples. As it turned out, you **don't** have to be Amish, **or** an artist, to make your own feather designs. After mastering just a few basic skills, you can create feather patterns for any quilt you want.

Since unlocking the door to feathering for myself, I have shared my abilities with students at quilting workshops across the country. Often, class participants enjoy drawing feathers so much I can hardly get them to stop feathering and go home! They leave class with the knowledge they need to create just the right quilting designs for the unfinished projects in their closets.

This book is designed to guide you through simple steps for making straight plumes, undulating plumes, feather borders any size, corners, circles, hearts and other fancies. The first section is devoted to a series of exercises that will give you a solid understanding of how feather motifs are formed. Then, in the second chapter, you'll learn to customize feather designs. The book also includes a discussion of techniques for marking designs on quilts, a chapter on actually quilting feathers, and a chapter on that ultimate goal for many dedicated quilters, the whole-cloth quilt. At the back of the book is a Treasury of feather designs you can adapt for your quilts. Several full size designs are given as well.

I encourage you to set aside a couple of days from your busy quilter's life and use them to work through the sections of this book. You'll gain long-lasting skills that can turn creating designs for quilting into your favorite step in the quiltmaking process.

Happy feathering,

Marianne

*Published by Yours Truly, Inc.

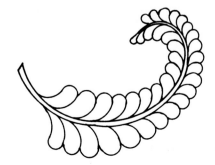

Feather Traditions

Feather motifs in needlework have probably been around since the first soldier who stuck an ostrich plume in his helmet to catch a lady's eye. As those gay plumes marched off to war and into storybook legends, the wives and sweethearts that were left behind stitched graceful reminders of their gallant knights.

The feather as a design motif was apparently established in England as early as the thirteenth century, when monks decorated the margins of their illustrated parchments with curling lines of feathers much like a quilter's undulating border design. Ornamental feathers became so popular that, in the fourteenth century, the Black Prince adopted a personal badge of three curled feathers that remains the official insignia of the Prince of Wales today. Mary, Queen of Scots, who idled away years in prison with exquisite embroideries, included a few feather designs among her works.

Feathers and Quilting

In the United States, we are so used to quilting combined with patchwork and applique we can easily forget that quilting by itself precedes the distinctive American patchwork or applique quilt by many centuries. Indeed, the practice of quilting plain cloth has a history in England that can be traced back to the sixteenth century. Two works on English quilting, **Traditional Quilting** by Mavis Fitzrandolph (1954), and **Quilting** by Averil Colby (1971), are illustrated primarily by all-quilted works. Most large pieces are medallions, i.e., they have a major central quilting motif surrounded by borders, though some are all-over patterns or border-like designs repeated in rows. Colby includes a photograph of a man's quilted linen cap from the seventeenth century. Its design of flower and stem-like motifs displays leaves that closely resemble the feather patterns we admire today.

"Linsey-woolsey" type quilts of the eighteenth century often displayed feather motifs, such as this circa 1772 wool quilt with homespun back. The quilt top, as well as the back, has many seams, even though the work would be categorized as a "whole-cloth" quilt. (Whole-cloth, 91" x 105", c. 1772, courtesy of Living History Farms, Des Moines, Iowa, photo by Kent Clawson.)

The all-quilted or whole-cloth quilt was apparently the fashionable bed-cover in England during the American colonial period. Such covers, made of wool, linen, cotton or various fiber combinations, were generally elaborately quilted, often with feather motifs.

According to Jonathan Holstein, in **The Pieced Quilt, an American Design Tradition** (1973), the first American quilts were very likely whole-cloth ones, the term whole-cloth indicating a coverlet made of a single length of extra wide fabric for each side. These early quilts are often called "linsey woolseys," a term that is rather confusing since it implies a fabric woven of linen and wool. Actually, according to Carleton L. Safford and Robert Bishop in **America's Quilts and Coverlets** (1980), the "linsey" part of the term derives from Lindsay, a village in Suffolk, England, the fabric's origin. Lindsay woolsey was apparently cloth of either cotton or linen woven with wool.

A feathering tour de force, this trapunto bedcover won first prize at the Chicago World's Fair in 1893. Quilts of this type, with stuffed feather motifs and lots of background quilting to throw the feathers into high relief, were often the master work of the nineteenth century quilter. The designs were sometimes needle-marked, or "scratched," since the quilter planned never to wash her finest quilt. She wanted no marks whatsoever on the surface fabric. (Trapunto quilt, 68″ x 66″, c. 1893, photo courtesy San Antonio Museum Association.)

Our early American ancestors made their quilts thick and large to warm themselves through hard winters, using fabric brought with them for the purpose, or material imported to the New World. They used the quilting designs popular in the Mother country at the time — representations of baskets, fruits, flowers, leaves, and, almost always, elaborate feathers. Soon, however, scarcity of large pieces of cloth forced women to sew narrower lengths of fabric together. As available pieces of fabric got smaller and smaller, the American patchwork quilt was born.

The inherited traditions of feather quilting continued to develop right alongside the new American patchwork quilt. In fact, the Tuels quilt (1785), which was cited by Jonathan Holstein as the earliest dated American quilt employing pieced work, has a wide outer border of plain cloth filled with curving quilted feather plumes. Indeed, feather quilting incorporated with patchwork as well as applique blocks can be found on quilts from every decade in American quilting history.

Rich feather quilting, used alone on plain fabric, was popular in the nineteenth century in the form of white work quilts. White work varieties are defined as coverlets made by quilting two pieces of fabric (one fine, one coarse) together, without batting, and then stuffing areas of the design with cotton, poking the loose cotton through the coarse weave fabric on the back with a stiletto. Trapunto versions used cording rather than loose cotton to raise the motifs. Candlewicking was also sometimes employed.

Exquisite examples of these styles have been published in **America's Quilts and Coverlets, New Discoveries in American Quilts** (1975), **19th Century Patchwork Quilt** (1983-84), and **Homage to Amanda** (1984). Some of them appear to be literally whole-cloth works, having no apparent seams on their front. Fantastic feather motifs are abundant within this quilt genre, although leaves, baskets and flowers often appear as well. Quite understandably, quilting designs on the white work quilts of the nineteenth century are more sophisticated and refined than the linsey-woolseys of an earlier time. Their makers probably constructed them under better conditions than the ladies who made linsey-woolseys, and the white works were made more as advanced exercises in needlework than as necessary bedding.

Historically, the whole-cloth quilts from the nineteenth century forward have often been the master work of an American quilter's career. The fineness of the quilting stitches themselves, and the patterns they delineate, carry the entire weight of the quilt's success. The fact that quite a few exquisite examples survive attests to their place as masterpieces, made more to display fine workmanship than to be used.

Although the Amish quilts of 1870-1950 are not literally wholecloth works, much that pertains to all-quilted quilts pertains to them too, since quilting designs are a major factor in their style. Wide cloth borders filled with curving plumes are trademarks of the best Amish quilts. One of the whole-cloth quilt designs in this book is Amish-inspired (see page 44), and a number of the motifs included in the **Treasury** section were drawn from Amish quilts.

As with any folk art tradition, feather patterns for quilting have been modified and added to as they passed from quilters in one community to another and from one generation to the next. During the great flowering of the American patchwork and applique quiltmaking tradition in the nineteenth century, quilters everywhere used feather designs, especially feather circles, to enhance the bold and beautiful surface designs of their quilts. Love of feather styles continued into the twentieth century.

Kansas artist Rose Kretsinger, whose quilts and quilting designs are unparallelled, wrote about feather designs in 1935:

"Perhaps the one ornamental motif most familiar to us in America and especially adaptable to quilting is the Ostrich Feather or Plume. It has always furnished inexhaustible areas for motif designs and bandings. The long slender center rib, bordered by segments of fronds, lends grace and beauty to mass arrangements of bandings. Variations of the feather have been used in wreath, scroll, band, wave, and medallions, large and small. Aside from its slender beauty, it offers less constructive difficulty than does the floral motif. After marking out the center rib, it is a simple matter to draw in the seg-

Fine feather quilting is virtually synonymous with the Pennsylvania Amish quilts of 1870-1950. This classic Center Diamond quilt displays a large feather ring in the diagonally-set center square as well as an undulating border plume that travels continuously around the quilt. Short sprays come from behind the curves of the main border plume to fill the wide border fabric. Instructions for customizing undulating border repeats are in Chapter 2. (Photo by Sharon Risedorph courtesy of The Esprit Quilt Collection, San Francisco.)

ments of fronds which make up the body of the plume. The feather has ever been given preference because it combines harmoniously with the patterns of patch or applique without losing sight of constructive strength of line or form of the quilt, filling in substantially the open undecorated spaces." (**The Romance of the Patchwork Quilt in America,** page 272)

While some quiltmakers might not agree that feather designs offer less constructive difficulty than other motifs, most of us would agree with what Kretsinger says about the classic beauty of feather patterns. By working through the chapters in this book, you'll soon come to agree with Kretsinger as feather designs become more accessible to you than any other kind of motif, and you become well able to add your own contributions to the traditions of fine feather quilting.

Kansas quilt artist extraordinare Rose Kretsinger created exquisite feather quilting designs that harmonize perfectly with the beautiful appliques of her Orchid Wreath quilt, one of nearly a dozen magnificent quilts she made between 1925-1933. Although Kretsinger did not do her own quilting, she designed and marked the patterns for her quilter to execute. A four-plumed Princess Feather-style motif was used in the center of the wreath while other sprays and fancies run to each side of the middle bias border. Instructions for customizing irregular shapes are in Chapter 2. (Orchid Wreath, 91½″ x 91″, 1928-1930. Photo courtesy Spencer Museum of Art, Lawrence, Kansas.)

Before You Begin

This book is organized to take you through a series of steps to the goal of customizing feather motifs for your quilts just as if you were a workshop student. The book will be most valuable to you if you follow the steps as they are presented. You will spend some time just **drawing** different kinds of feather motifs before you work with applying them to quilts. First you will practice and understand straight plumes, then undulating ones. You will go on to drawing a feather circle and heart. Instructions for precisely fitting different kinds of designs on your quilts and for transferring designs to cloth follow the hands-on drawing exercises. By the time you reach the back of the book, where more feather ideas are presented, you will know how to adapt any of them for your own projects. For best results, don't skip ahead. Work through the book in the order presented. Each step is a prerequisite for the next.

The exercises are printed on separate sheets for ease in tracing. Carefully remove them by opening the staples and lifting the sheets out. Push the ends of the staples down again to keep your book intact.

To work the exercises, you'll need good tracing paper (11″ x 17″ sheets will match the printed design sheets), pencils, eraser and a clear plastic ruler.

Chapter I: Basic Feathering, Drawing Exercises

Feathering designs are made up of a series of overlapping scallop shapes. The first step in learning to draw feather motifs is to understand this simple scallop shape and practice drawing it until you find yourself automatically doodling rows of feathers on the backs of envelopes while chatting on the phone.

Think of the scallop shape as half of a common Valentine heart (Figure 1), the kind everyone has drawn at some time. In exercise A (separate exercise sheet), some of the feathers are already drawn in. Notice that the top side of the straight plume is made up of "right-hand" sides of hearts, and the bottom side of the plume is made up of "left-hand" sides of hearts. (You may need to turn the sheet upside down to see this.) When drawing feather motifs, you will draw both right and left sides of hearts. Notice also, that the half-heart scallop shape consists of a "hump" and a "tail" (Figure 2). The tail always ends up roughly just below the starting point of the hump.

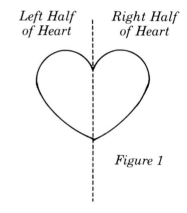

Left Half of Heart   *Right Half of Heart*

Figure 1

Most feather designs have a center vein. If you think of a real bird's feather, this center vein would represent the hard center quill of the feather. A feather quilting design can have a single or double center vein. Some old quilts even have triple center vein lines. Double (or triple) lines are especially beautiful when quilted because the lines of stitching raise the narrow area between them, making the vein appear stuffed, or trapuntoed (corded). Exercises A and B have simple single center vein lines. Exercise C has a split vein with a design in the middle. Exercises D and E have double veins.

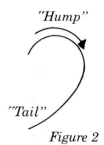

"Hump"

"Tail"

Figure 2

Another key element in a feather motif is the outer guideline or guidelines. These lines (imaginary, on the quilt) delineate the area that is filled with feathers. The outer guidelines on exercise A are drawn 1½″ to each side of the center vein. Thus the design will be 3″ wide. Exercise B has outer guidelines drawn just 1″ to each side of the center vein, forming a 2″ wide plume. As you work through this book, you'll learn that establishing outer guidelines is always an important step in forming feather motifs.

One last element must be noted before you go to the first drawing exercises. As you can see, several of the half-heart shapes are already drawn to each side of the center vein in exercise A. Even where the feathering leaves off, a series of small scallops (the "humps") continues next to the outer guideline on the upper half of the feather all the way to the end of the line. These partial hearts were made using a coin (in this case, a quarter) as a template. These pre-drawn scallops will help you draw the feathers. You will use various-size coins and other "household templates" in the drawing exercises ahead. Later, when you are ready to mark feathering designs on cloth, you will make your own special templates to use.

Straight Plumes

In my feathering workshop, students receive class handout sheets very much like the ones in this book. The students are always asked to lay tracing paper over each printed sheet so they can practice feathering without marking on the handout. This way, they can do the exercise as many times as they want, just by replacing the tracing paper as needed.

Lay a piece of tracing paper over exercise A. Using a pencil and ruler, first trace the center vein and outer guidelines onto the paper. Next, trace the top row of feathers that are already drawn on the sheet. The little arrows show you the direction in which to draw. When you run out of pre-drawn feathers, continue drawing right sides of hearts, using the partial scallops to help you as you work to the end of the line. Trace over each hump, then bring the tail down into the center vein so that you are drawing the entire half heart shape each time. Keep in mind that the hump of each feather should be plump, round and smooth. The individual feather shape should be round enough at the top so that a coin could actually fit in it. As the line comes down to the center vein, it should curve gently every bit of the way, and the tail of the feather should merge into the center vein smoothly and naturally, like a real feather.

After drawing the top row of feathers, which you did by making right sides of hearts, complete the other side of the center vein by drawing left sides of hearts. Notice that the helpful partial scallops are missing on this side. Use a quarter to draw in these scallops on your tracing paper. When drawing with the coin template, be sure to keep the edge of the coin just **inside** the outer guideline. Also be sure to draw enough of the coin's curve. Draw almost the whole top half of the coin, not just a narrow arc.

When drawing the bottom side of the plume, you may want to experiment with turning your paper at various angles to find your own most comfortable position for working. Turning the page straight out in front of you may be best. Left-handed people sometimes turn their exercise sheet completely around for a comfortable angle. However you angle the paper, the little arrows will show the direction for drawing the half-hearts.

It's not fair simply to move the tracing paper and keep tracing the feathers printed on the sheet, nor are you allowed to fold the paper in half on the center vein and copy your top row for the bottom.

When drawing the lower side of the plume, **don't try to make the tails of the feathers on each side meet along the center vein**. They look better offset, and, besides, when you go on to undulating plumes, you'll find it's impossible to make tails meet. When using a coin to make scallop guidelines, slightly offset the humps on opposite sides of the center vein.

Also, don't try to make each half-heart look exactly alike. Study pictures of antique quilts and you will see how randomness in feather quilting designs contributes much to their beauty. Many quilters are admitted perfectionists, and, when it comes to patchwork, insisting on perfect accuracy is definitely a virtue. When approaching quilting designs, however, relax a bit. An eighth or quarter-inch error in patchwork spells disaster, but if a quilting design shifts a little here or there, no one is likely to notice. So, don't use your ruler to measure every single feather in order to make them all exactly the same size — you don't want your feathers to look stamped out by a machine.

After you have completed exercise A once, get a fresh piece of tracing paper and do the exercise a second time. The feathers become easier the more you draw. The box on Insert #1 describes some common problems. Study these potential errors and check your work against them.

Exercise B shows the scallops starting at the right side of the page and flowing to the left. In this case, left sides of hearts are on the top side of the center vein, and right sides of hearts are on the bottom. The outer guidelines are just 1″ from the center vein, and the helping scallops were made with a penny as a template.

Lay tracing paper over example B and complete the exercise. Remember to trace the center vein onto your paper first. Tracing the outer guidelines is optional, since you can see them as you work. In this exercise, right-handed people may find they need to turn the sheet in order to draw comfortably. You'll need your own penny to make the helping scallops for the top side of the plume. Notice the little arrows that suggest you draw the humps first, then the tail. Some students find they make better half-hearts if they draw the tail first, starting at the center vein and sketching their way up into the hump. Experiment to find what works best for you. Do exercise B a second or third time if you feel you need more practice.

Exercise C has simple small feathers on each side of a split double vein. Little 1″ hearts fill the space. Use a dime to scallop guidelines. Complete exercise C.

More Practice on Straight Plumes

In exercise D, outer guidelines are 2″ away from the double center vein, making a 4″ wide design. A regular size thread spool makes a good scalloping template for large feathers like these. Notice how a heart or teardrop shape can be used at any point along a plume to reverse the direction of the feathers. The heart and teardrop will come in handy when you plan borders and corner turns for quilts. Again, use tracing paper over the printed sheet when you do exercise D. Trace the center vein, make the guiding partial scallops, and draw the feathers to the end of the lines on each side.

In the straight plume variation E, the center vein is a double one, and the outer guidelines get wider and narrower along the plume. A dime was used as a template to make the scalloping lines. You will learn to form your own undulating lines in later exercises. For now, use the scalloped outer guideline to complete the two sides of the plume.

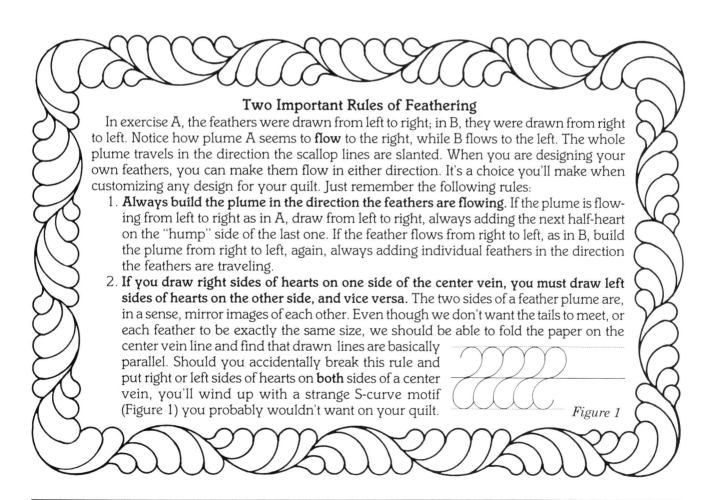

Two Important Rules of Feathering

In exercise A, the feathers were drawn from left to right; in B, they were drawn from right to left. Notice how plume A seems to **flow** to the right, while B flows to the left. The whole plume travels in the direction the scallop lines are slanted. When you are designing your own feathers, you can make them flow in either direction. It's a choice you'll make when customizing any design for your quilt. Just remember the following rules:

1. **Always build the plume in the direction the feathers are flowing.** If the plume is flowing from left to right as in A, draw from left to right, always adding the next half-heart on the "hump" side of the last one. If the feather flows from right to left, as in B, build the plume from right to left, again, always adding individual feathers in the direction the feathers are traveling.

2. **If you draw right sides of hearts on one side of the center vein, you must draw left sides of hearts on the other side, and vice versa.** The two sides of a feather plume are, in a sense, mirror images of each other. Even though we don't want the tails to meet, or each feather to be exactly the same size, we should be able to fold the paper on the center vein line and find that drawn lines are basically parallel. Should you accidentally break this rule and put right or left sides of hearts on **both** sides of a center vein, you'll wind up with a strange S-curve motif (Figure 1) you probably wouldn't want on your quilt.

Figure 1

Undulating Plumes

Feather plumes that wind back and forth make beautiful border quilting designs. In exercises F, G, H and I, you will learn to draw feathers on curving lines. In Chapter II, you'll learn to form and customize undulating curves for your own quilt projects. Looking at exercise F on the printed insert sheet, notice the hills and valleys formed opposite each other by the winding center vein.

The main difference you will find when you begin drawing half-hearts on curving, rather than straight, center veins is that the successive individual **feather tails will be spaced further apart when you dip down into a valley than they are when you work up onto a hill.** Drawing the half-hearts in the valley areas sometimes seems awkward because of this different spacing. To understand how this wider spacing occurs, study Figure 1 on this page. It represents an undulating center vein and outer guidelines.

Notice how, when the center vein dips down in a valley, there is more space to be filled along

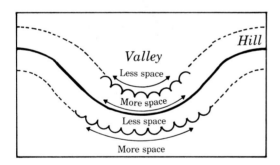

Figure 1

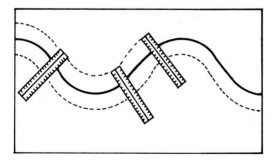

Figure 2

the vein than at the outer guideline. Only a few feather humps will fit on the outer line, and the tails of those few humps must be spread out along the center vein.

On the hill, the outer guideline is longer than the center vein, so there is plenty of room for the round humps of the feathers. The tails curve easily down to fill the shorter center vein area.

Look carefully at the feathers drawn in the valley area of exercise F. Notice that the individual feathers are still just normal half-hearts. Some dotted lines have been drawn on a few of the half-hearts from the starting point of the hump down to the tail to show this. The tails end pretty much under the starting point of the. humps. It's the increased spacing that makes the half-hearts look elongated. When drawing each half-heart along a curving center vein, keep the heart shape in mind and curve the tail portion of the line into the center vein as gracefully as possible. Practice will make it easy. Look at the tabard photo opposite to see how pretty these longer-looking feathers can be on a quilt.

To do exercise F, lay tracing paper over the whole length of the plume, just as you have done in the earlier exercises. First, copy the center vein onto your paper. Lightly sketch in the outer guidelines too. Start drawing the plume by tracing over the feathers that are already drawn for you on the top side of the center vein. Where they leave off, the small partial scallops continue. Use them to help you continue feathering to the end of the center vein, but be sure you draw each entire half-heart — don't just draw the tail. On the other side of the vein, the outer guideline has been printed, but you will have to make your own guiding scallops. Use a dime to draw scallops all along the outer guideline of the lower side of the plume, keeping the edge of the coin just touching the outer guideline. Complete the feathers. The top side of the plume is made up of right sides of hearts, so the bottom will have to be left sides of hearts. **(See Important Rule #2, page 11.)**

When you were making straight plumes in exercises A-E, you were advised to offset the humps of the individual feathers so that the tails would not meet along the center vein. Notice that when you are working with curving center veins, the tails are automatically offset. This is because the number of individual feathers increases and decreases along the hills and valleys on opposite sides of the center line. If tails occasionally meet on plumes like this, don't worry about it. Your feathers will still have a natural, organic look. Do exercise F more than once if you like.

To work through exercise G, you will need a piece of tracing paper as long as the center vein shown and about 6″ wide. First, trace the center vein on your paper. Now the outer guidelines must be added. Care must be taken when drawing outer guidelines for undulating veins. Note how, in exercise F, the outer guideline is EXACTLY 1″ out from the vein on each side all along its length. If you are careless in your measuring during this step, and allow the guideline to be wider in some spots and narrower in others, you'll have trouble when drawing the individual feathers. For exercise G, make the outer guidelines 1½" away from the center vein. A clear plastic ruler is a good tool for this procedure. Figure 2 shows how to turn your ruler perpendicular to the curving vein. Make a small mark exactly 1½" out from the vein every so often. Connect the marks lightly with pencil to form the outer guideline. Draw guidelines on both sides of the center vein.

Next you need to use a coin (a quarter, for exercise G) to make the partial scallops just inside or against the outer guidelines. If you are beginning to feel fairly proficient at making the individual feather scallops, you may want to try freehanding them without a coin.

A decision you must make now is whether this plume G is going to flow from left to right or right to left. If you want it to flow from left to right, start drawing at the left side of the paper and make right sides of hearts on the top and left hearts on the bottom. If you want the plume to flow from right to left, start your work at the right side of the page. Draw left sides of hearts on the top side of the center vein and right sides of hearts on the bottom. For extra practice, you could do the exercise twice, first with the plume flowing one way, and the second time flowing the opposite direction.

TABARD. The deep horseshoe-shape feather corner often seen on classic Amish quilts inspired the feathering on this quilted tabard. The design was worked out on paper the exact finished size of the garment, then traced onto the cloth. Diagonal lines form background quilting that enhances the main motif. (Tabard, 20" x 22", made by Marianne Fons, using a pattern by Yvonne Porcella.)

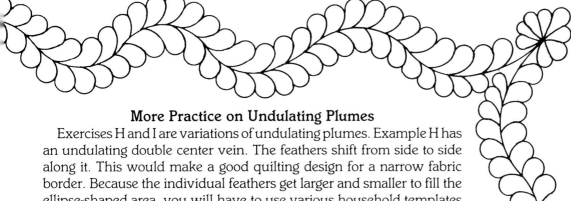

More Practice on Undulating Plumes

Exercises H and I are variations of undulating plumes. Example H has an undulating double center vein. The feathers shift from side to side along it. This would make a good quilting design for a narrow fabric border. Because the individual feathers get larger and smaller to fill the ellipse-shaped area, you will have to use various household templates (small buttons and coins) to make guiding scallops along the dotted line if you need them. Or, try working without templates on this one. Complete the individual feathers within the dotted line areas as shown. Be sure to put tracing paper over the sheet before drawing.

Exercise I is a classic double undulating plume that would be used for a fairly wide fabric border. In such a border, the two plumes weave over and under one another as they travel around the quilt. In Chapter II, you will learn to create this design in any size for your own quilts. You'll learn to make such borders fit your quilt perfectly, travel around it with no break, and have all four corners alike. For now, just practice drawing the feathers. Use a dime for a template to make guiding scallops just inside the dashed outer guidelines for both plumes. Use tracing paper over the printed sheet.

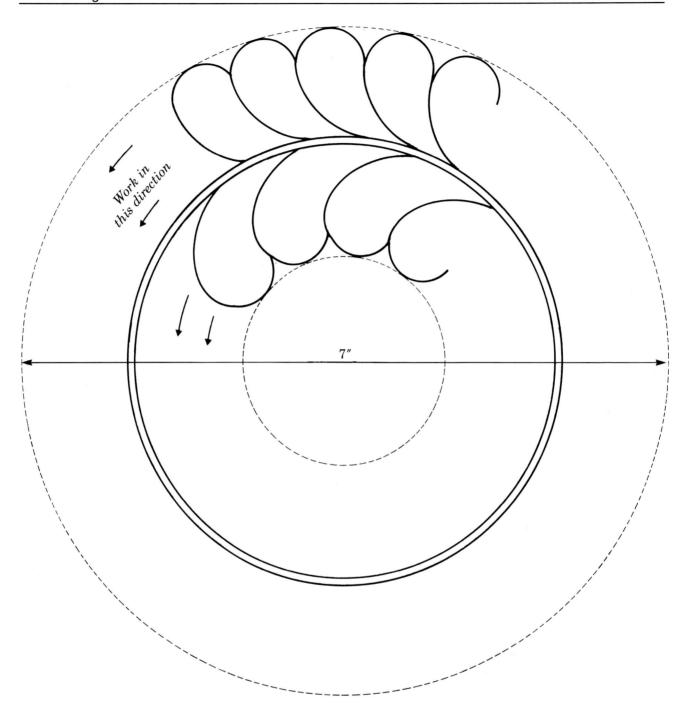

7"

Work in this direction

Circle

Feather circles, also called feather rings, are perhaps the most beautiful and best-loved quilting designs in the history of quilting. They are ideal for filling in plain blocks in applique as well as patchwork quilts. Feather rings really aren't hard to draw, especially with the experience you have gained by completing exercises A-I.

In Chapter II, you will learn to make feather rings any size you want. Several circle variations are shown on pages 31 and 55. For now, you should simply study the following comments about circles and complete the drawing exercise as directed.

Looking at the few feathers already drawn in on the circle above, notice that they flow in a **counter-clockwise** (to the left) direction. That's because left sides of hearts were drawn to the outside of the center vein and right sides of hearts were drawn to the inside of the vein. If you wanted a circle that flowed **clockwise** (to the right), you would put right sides of hearts to the outside and left sides of hearts to the inside.

On page 11, under "Two Important Rules," the first rule was "always build the plume in the direction the feathers are flowing." The arrows in the circle above are to remind you of this rule.

Lay tracing paper over the page. Trace the center vein. Use a penny as a template to make guiding scallops just inside the dashed outer guidelines on both sides of the center vein. As you get back to the starting place, you may have to erase a few scallops, and squeeze or stretch a few humps slightly to complete the outer scallops to your satisfaction.

Notice that there will be many more feathers to the outside than the inside. The outer ring is like one continuous "hill" while the inner ring is one continuous "valley." Thus the spaces between the tails will be wider for the inner ring. This extra space will make the half-heart shapes of the inner ring look like extended commas or like comets, even though they are still normal half-hearts. Make the tails flow smoothly into the center vein on both sides as you feather the circle. For extra practice, you could make a clockwise circle after you have completed the one above.

Heart

Not just for Valentines, the heart motif has had its place in the decorative arts for centuries. Feather hearts have long been stitched into wedding and friendship quilts to signify love.

In Chapter II, you'll learn to make feather hearts any size you need for your quilting projects. For now, just study this heart design as well as the following comments about its construction; then complete the drawing exercise as directed.

The two halves of a heart design are true mirror images. When originating a feather heart of your own, you'll only draw one side of it, then fold the paper and draw the other half, an exact reverse. In drawing exercise K (see insert sheet), only the center vein, the outer guidelines on the right side of the heart and the small heart/teardrop at the top of the design are provided. The heart/teardrop is the starting point for the scallops that make the heart. Use a nickel to create helping humps just inside the guidelines to each side of the center vein. Refer to the sketch of the completed heart at right as needed. As with the feather circle, many more individual feathers will be to the outside than to the inside of the heart. The outside is like a continuous hill, the inside a tight, continuous valley. The tails of all the half-heart scallops should still end up just below the starting point of the humps. The feather scallops will still be normal half-heart shapes. Because the inside area of the heart is small, only a few feather humps will fit there. The tails of these humps must be spread out over a fairly long center vein area. This increased spacing makes the feather scallops appear lengthened or extended.

To do the heart drawing exercise, first fold a piece of tracing paper in half. Open it out and lay it over the drawing on Insert #2, aligning the fold with the dashed center line of the feather heart. Trace the top heart/teardrop, the center vein and the outer guidelines onto your paper. Use a nickel to create helping humps just inside the guidelines to each side of the center vein on the right side of the heart. Complete each half-heart scallop, bringing the tail gently into the center vein. Refer to the small heart sketch as needed. Once you are satisfied with the right side of the heart, fold the paper back and trace the left side of the design.

Having completed this exercise and the preceding ones in this chapter, you are ready to go on to the next chapter, where you will learn to adapt any feather design for your own projects.

Chapter II: Customizing Feather Motifs

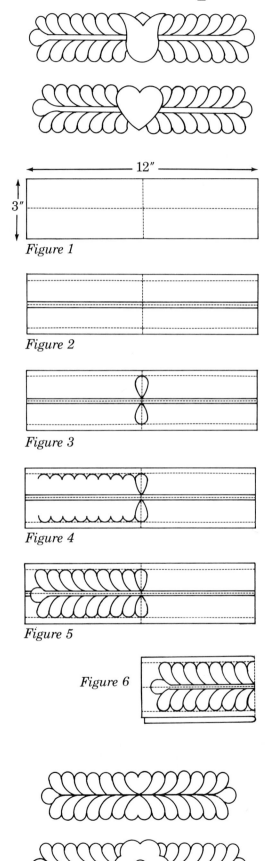

Figure 1

Figure 2

Figure 3

Figure 4

Figure 5

Figure 6

The drawing exercises you did in Chapter I familiarized you with the basic shapes and elements of feather motifs. Now you are ready to learn techniques for customizing those motifs for your own projects.

If you've ever looked through a book of full size quilting designs in search of one you could use, you know how important it is to visualize the design on the quilt. You probably held the printed pattern close to the area to be quilted to see if the design would be appropriate. You may have even traced it and then placed the tracing on your quilt top. It's easy, then, to understand that **quilting designs must always be worked out on paper first** to let you visualize them on your quilt. In working through exercises A-K, you probably used up a quantity of tracing paper. This semi-transparent paper you can trace through and fold easily, continues to be your best friend when adapting designs for your quilts and other projects.

In this chapter, you will see how to use pencil and tracing paper to make any feather design the size you need.

Customizing Straight Plumes

Straight plumes are natural fillers for sashings and border strips. They can also be adapted to fill other shapes.

A Simple Sashing Plume. To make a straight plume pattern for a simple sashing strip, first cut a piece of tracing paper the **exact** size of the fabric strip you want to fill with quilting. The example at left is a sashing strip that will finish 3" x 12". Fold the paper strip in half horizontally and vertically to form center guidelines. Unfold (Figure 1).

So that feathers will not crowd the seam area, draw outer guidelines ¼" to ½" **in** from the cut edges of the paper on the two long sides. For a single center vein, just draw a line on the horizontal fold. If you want a double center vein, draw a line 1/8" (or less) to each side of the horizontal fold (Figure 2).

If you like using a coin to scallop your outer guidelines, select one that seems a good size to you. Center the coin for the first guiding humps. Make a hump on each side of the center vein, just inside the outer guideline. Extend the semi-circle to form teardrops directly across from each other (Figure 3). Use the coin to scallop the rest of the outer guidelines on the right half of the plume, offsetting the scallops slightly so that tails won't meet (Figure 4). Complete feathers on the left half of the plume, ending as shown in Figure 5, leaving enough space at the end of the design not to crowd the seam. Erase the part of the center vein that goes into the ending bump.

Fold the blank half of the paper **back** so you can see the completed half of the plume through it (Figure 6). Trace the design onto the paper so you will have a balanced mirror image design.

You can follow the same steps for sashings on a quilt of your own just by making the strip of tracing paper the size you need. Variations on straight plume ideas are shown here and in the **Treasury** appendix at the back of the book.

Be Sure You Understand "Design Area"

The design area is the portion of the fabric actually covered by the design (eventually, the quilting stitches). Just as a printed page needs margins and a beautiful drawing needs a mat, quilting designs need "air" around them to enhance their beauty and effectiveness. Determining how much margin is needed is an important part of the customizing process.

Study old quilts and you will see that our quilting friends of 100 years ago sometimes had problems with design area. Many a fine antique quilt has feather rings too large for the squares they fill. The outer scallops of the ring are crowded right up next to the seams or, sometimes, disappear right into them! Quilting patterns too small for their design area seem to be a more modern phenomenon, caused, in part, by the widespread acceptance of stabilized polyester batting. In the old days, when loose cotton batting was used, every inch of a quilt had to be quilted, either with a fancy motif or a grid. Nowadays, we sometimes see a new quilt, with setting squares, perhaps, whose too-small quilting motif is floating lonesomely in the middle of the square. The old-time quilter left not enough margin; the contemporary quilter tends to leave too much. Generally speaking, allow ½" to 1" margin between your quilting motif and a fabric edge or seam. Thus a 12" finished block might have a feather circle whose outer diameter is 10½", leaving ¾" of margin on each side. Making the quilting design smaller than a fabric block or border strip prevents the quilting motif from dipping into seams and also keeps the viewer's eye undistracted. Indeed, your block, border or other area may also have a grid or have background filler quilting that appears to run behind the major quilting motif. See how the grid works behind the central motif of the Princess Feather whole-cloth quilt, pictured on page 25. This filler quilting can, and often should, cover the entire fabric area, reaching and even crossing seams. It, too, enhances the beauty of feathered or other primary quilting designs. Several background quilting options are illustrated on insert sheet #4.

OCEAN WAVES. The feather twist design is just right for filling the diagonally-placed setting squares of the Ocean Waves scrap quilt. Smaller V-shaped plume designs fill the setting triangles along the sides and the corner triangles. The quilt's middle border has a continuous feather plume whose center vein undulates while the outer quideline stays even with the seam. The individual feather scallops are lengthened or shortened as needed to fill the border. (Ocean Waves Scrap Quilt, 80" x 100", made by Liz Porter and Marianne Fons, quilted by Helen Martens. This quilt first appeared in **Creative Ideas for Living,** September, 1986.)

This heart is too big   *This heart is too small*   *This heart is just right*

Straight Plumes to Fill a Square

Let's say you want to use a quilting design like the one shown here for the plain fabric blocks in a quilt. The blocks are 12″ finished size. First, you must subtract margin space from that 12″ square. (See Design Area, page 17.) Allowing ½″ of margin on each side of the square makes a design area 11″ x 11″.

Measure and cut an 11″ square of tracing paper. Fold it vertically and horizontally to make center guidelines. Also draw or fold diagonal lines from corner to corner each way.

Start the feathering by drawing a heart as shown in Figure 1. Draw a line in the crease to make a center vein; then draw in the feathers along the vein as shown in Figure 2. Work to the very edge of the paper since it represents the design area for the pattern. Make a semi-circle at the end of the plume. Darken the heart, center vein, and feathers with pencil or black marker.

Now fold the top half of the paper down and trace the design onto the bottom half (Figure 3). Then fold the paper in half diagonally and trace the design onto the left side of the paper (Figure 4). Flip the paper over to draw the design on the right side of the paper. The vertical-horizontal cross of straight feathers is now complete (Figure 5).

To make the diagonal cross of feathers, draw that part of the design in one of the four empty quadrants of the paper as shown in Figure 6. Fold and trace as needed to complete the design.

Take a look at the straight plume variations in the Treasury appendix and the insert sheets. You can adapt any of them for your own quilt projects simply by starting with a piece of tracing paper the size of the design area for which you wish to create a quilting motif. Fold, sketch, refold and flip the paper in order to make complete designs. In Chapter III, you'll learn ways to transfer designs to cloth.

Customizing Undulating Plumes for Border Designs

Wide fabric borders figure importantly in Amish quilts, often filled with exquisite curving feather designs. Quilters making other styles of quilts, whether patchwork, applique or a combination, often choose fabric borders to bring their quilt top to the size they want and to give their work a proper frame. Instructions that follow will teach you how to form undulating feather quilting designs that flow around entire border with no break.

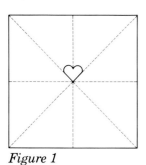

Figure 1

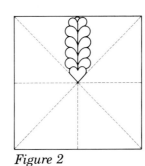

Figure 2

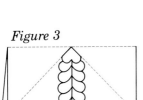

Figure 3

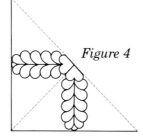

Figure 4

Figure 5

Figure 6

How to Form a Repeat

Look back at exercise F on insert 2. Notice the dashed vertical lines labeled "repeat line." The center vein between those lines is an elongated U-shape. This shape, also drawn at right (Figure 1), is the basic repeat unit that is placed end to end with others just like it to form continuous undulating plumes. You will probably recognize its hill and valley areas from the drawing exercises in Chapter I.

1. Use a rectangular piece of tracing paper. It should be at least twice as long as it is wide, but the exact size isn't important for this exercise. (If you've been using 11" x 17" sheets to work the exercises in this book, you can just cut or tear a piece in half lengthwise and use one of the halves.)

2. Fold the strip of paper in half twice, to make three vertical folds as shown in Figure 2. Open the paper out again.

3. Fold the strip of paper in half twice the other way, to form three horizontal folds as shown in Figure 3. Open the paper out. You should have 16 small boxes, four columns of four rectangular boxes each.

4. In the far left column, second box from the top, draw a smooth curving line from the top left corner of the box to the lower right corner of the box as shown in Figure 4. Darken the curved line with pencil or black marking pen.

5. Fold the left half of the paper **back,** so that the cuved line you drew in Step 4 shows through in the second box from the top on the far right column (Figure 5). Trace the curved line and darken it. When you open the paper out again, it will look like Figure 6.

6. To complete the repeat shape, the paper must be folded again, and the curved line drawn in the lower middle portion of the paper rectangle to form the valley area. To avoid confusion when the paper is folded, make a little "x" in the third box from the top in the middle two columns as shown in Figure 6.

7. Fold the far left and far right columns **back** as shown in Figure 7. Then fold the top half of the paper **back** and **down,** as shown in Figure 8, so that the curves you drew in Steps 4 and 5 show through the two boxes marked with "x"s. Trace the curve into these boxes.

8. When you open out the paper, you will see the basic repeat unit shape, a smooth undulating curve like Figure 1.

Repeats like this can be placed end to end to form the center vein for continuous feather borders. Whether an odd or an even number of these units are used, the repeat lines will enter the corner consistently. Work through the exercise on page 22 to see how to customize this repeat unit for borders in your own quilts.

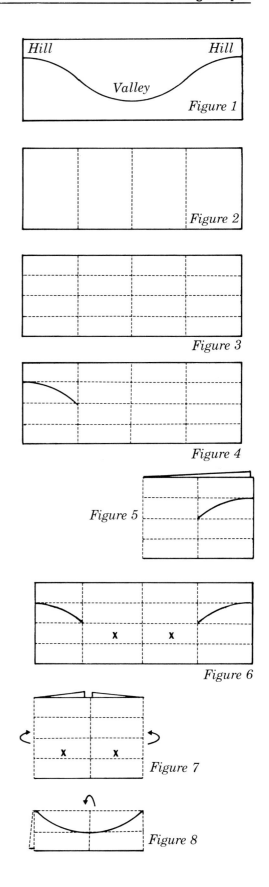

Figure 1

Figure 2

Figure 3

Figure 4

Figure 5

Figure 6

Figure 7

Figure 8

IOWA STAR QUILT. The center vein of the diamond-shaped feather motif used in this fullsize quilt is the seam that joins the Iowa Star blocks. Shades of blue, graduating from light in the center to dark at the outer edges, were used to emphasize the circular effect achieved by combining the star blocks. This quilt is a good illustration of how appropriate feather designs can be for patchwork quilts. (Iowa Star, 78″ x 104″, designed by Liz Porter and Marianne Fons, top made by members of Heritage Quilters of Winterset, Iowa, quilted by Luella Fairholm.)

BOSTON COMMONS. Simple straight-feather plumes were used to fill the 4″ wide muslin borders of this Boston Commons crib quilt. The plumes are 3″ wide to allow margin to each side of the quilting. Exercises in drawing straight plumes are included in Chapter I, customizing instructions are in Chapter II. (Boston Commons, 44″ x 38″, made by Marianne Fons.)

TRUE LOVER'S KNOT. The true lover's knot typical of English North Country quilting was enlarged many times and filled with gorgeous feathers to provide a central motif for this whole-cloth quilt. Dark blue on one side and pale blue on the reverse, this quilt also has classic feathered double hearts in the inner area and interwoven plumes for an outer border. A two-inch grid fills most of the background of the quilt, with smaller grids in the hearts and loops of the knot. Full instructions for making this quilt are in Chapter V. (True Lover's Knot, 80″ x 100″, designed and made by Liz Porter.)

How to Customize a Repeat Unit

The diagram below shows a quilt whose center portion is 63″ wide and 88″ long. The fabric borders are 12″ wide. Notice that these borders are mitered at the corners, but dashed lines are drawn to show that, **when figuring border repeats, the corner is a separate unit, a square.** The size of the side borders, then is 12″ wide by 88″ long. The end borders are 12″ wide by 63″ long.

Keeping in mind what you learned about design area on page 17, you know that the border motif will need margins to each side so the quilting will not dip into seams. Allowing a 1″ margin on each side of the example border strip gives a design width of 10″.

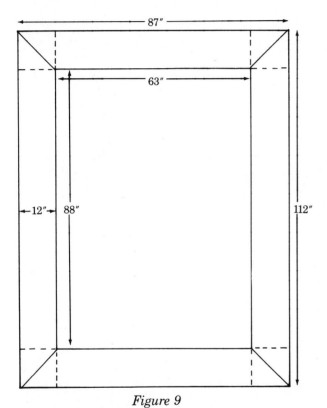

Figure 9

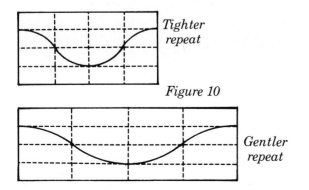

Tighter repeat

Figure 10

Gentler repeat

Now that you know the design width, you need to determine the repeat length. The rule of thumb is: **the approximate repeat length is the design width times two.** In this example, multiply the design width of 10″ times two to get an **approximate** repeat length of 20″.

Now we know that a repeat unit length of about 20″ will work on the border. Before we can determine the **exact** repeat lengths for side and end borders, we must figure out how many repeats will fit in each border. Divide the **approximate** repeat length (20″) into the side border length and then into the end border length. Round the fraction off to the nearest whole number.

Side Border
     88″ ÷ 20″ = 4 2/5 repeats
     (Round off to 4 repeats.)

End Border
     63″ ÷ 20″ = 3 3/20 repeats
     (Round off to 3 repeats.)

Now we know that the side borders will have four repeats and the end border will have three repeats.

To determine **exact** repeat length for side borders, divide four (for four repeats) into the border length (88 ÷ 4 = 22″). The **exact** side border repeat length is 22″. For exact end border repeat length, divide three (for three repeats) into the border length (63″ ÷ 3 = 21″). The **exact** end border repeat length is 21″.

Now you are ready to use the paper folding techniques you learned on page 19 to form the two border repeats. For the side border repeat, your tracing paper will be 10″ x 22″. For the end border repeat, your tracing paper will be 10″ x 21″. For each of these two papers, follow Steps 1-7 on page 19. If you were working with a square quilt, just one repeat length would work for all four sides.

If after folding paper and drawing your repeats, you feel that your repeat curves look too tight, you can form a gentler repeat. Simply work through the steps for forming repeats again (use the Reference Box on page 23) but determine the approximate repeat length by multiplying the design width by **three** instead of two (Figure 10).

Be aware that the repeats you create for side borders and end borders are not identical, but they are usually close enough to **appear** identical on a completed quilt. Once you have formed the two different tracing paper repeats, be sure to label them "side" and "end" so you won't get them mixed up. Of course, if you are working on a square quilt, just one repeat will work for all sides.

Chapter III will show you how to make templates for transferring your repeats to cloth.

A Few Words About Placing Repeats in Borders

The repeat unit you have learned to form can be placed in a border one of two ways. As you'll learn in the section on corners that follows, the way you place the repeat will affect the style of corner design available to you. Understanding the two placement options is a key to working with repeats.

The repeat has been described as an extended U-shape, and, in the repeat-forming exercise, you became accustomed to viewing it that way. Recalling the drawing exercises you did for undulating plumes in Chapter I, the repeat illustrated in Figure 11 above could also be thought of as a valley with partial hills to each side. Note that this same repeat unit can be flipped over (Figure 12). Then it becomes a hill with partial valleys to each side. With either type of placement, even or odd numbers of these units can be placed end to end to travel around a quilt. Once you decide whether you want the hill or the valley placed to the inside of the quilt, you must place the repeat the selected way consistently. Interwoven repeats, which will be discussed on page 28, are formed when the repeat unit is used both ways at once (Figure 13).

As noted already, these repeat units can be combined in even or odd numbers in quilt borders. Sometimes, the side borders may require an even number of repeats, while the end borders need an odd number. When the repeat is used an odd number of times in a border, the center point of the repeat line must match up with the center point of the quilt border (Figure 14).

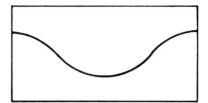

Figure 11

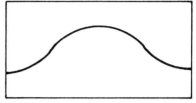

Figure 12

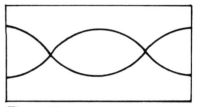

Figure 13

Figure 14

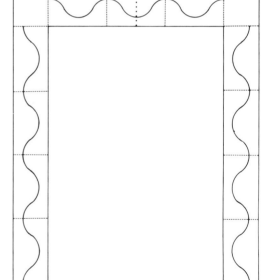

For odd numbers of repeats, center the repeat at border mid-point

---

Reference Box for Forming Border Repeats

1. Determine length of borders, excluding corners.
2. Determine design width by allowing ½″ to 1″ margin to each side of design.
3. Determine **approximate** repeat length by multiplying design width by two. (If repeats seem too tight, try an approximate repeat length **three** times wider than width instead of **two**.)
4. Determine number of repeats that will fit in border by dividing border length by approximate repeat length.
5. Find **exact** repeat length by dividing border length by number of repeats.
6. Fold paper to form repeats.

Note: Exact repeat length may not always be a nice even number. An alternate method for finding repeat size is to work just through Step 4. Once you know the number of repeats the border will have, use a piece of adding machine tape the length of the border (excluding corners) and simply fold it into the needed number of repeats. Use the folded repeat length to "measure" and cut your tracing paper. You don't really need to know the mathematical measurement of the repeat.

AMISH BARS. The zigzag setting of the blocks in this Amish Bars quilt was inspired by a photo of an antique Amish quilt in a calendar. The feather plume that meanders through the plain black triangles of the blocks is made up of half and quarter circles. By following the instructions in the book, you can make feather circles any size. (Amish Bars, 45" x 60", made by Marianne Fons, quilted by Lois Wilson.)

TREE WALL QUILTS. Both of these tree pattern wall quilts have undulating feather plumes in their fabric borders. The border quilting in the Tree of Life shows up well on the solid ivory fabric. The curving design in the border of the Tree of Paradise is hidden by the blue-gray print. A small teardrop and feather motif fills the ivory print setting triangles next to the tree block. (Tree of Life, 37" x 37", and Tree of Paradise, 30" x 30", by Marianne Fons.)

PRINCESS FEATHER. Inspiration for the Princess Feather's central motif, as well as its corner scrolls, came from a drawing in **The Romance of the Patchwork Quilt in America** by Carrie A. Hall and Rose G. Kretsinger (p. 275). This quilt, made of two shades of lavendar, combines the two interior motifs with an interwoven feather/cable border. One-inch and two-inch grids set off the feather designs. Full instructions for making this quilt are in Chapter V. (Princess Feather, 78″ x 98″, designed and made by Marianne Fons.)

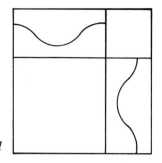

Figure 1

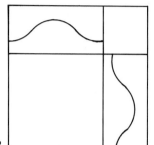

Figure 2

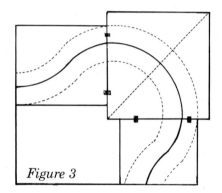

Figure 3

How to Make Corners for Undulating Border Plumes

When planning your own undulating feather borders, one of the decisions you will need to make, once you've formed your repeat, is how the repeat line is going to enter the corner. The type of corner designs available to you will be affected by your decision. Remember that, from a design standpoint, the corner is always a separate unit, a square.

A border repeat can be positioned on the border and enter the corner square in either of two ways. In Figure 1, the repeat is entering the corner area with the repeat line/center vein curving to the **outside** edge of the quilt. Figure 2 shows the repeat line entering the corner with the repeat line/center vein curving to the **inside** of the quilt. Regardless of whether your border requires an even or an odd number of repeats, once you've chosen the way you want the repeat positioned, all the corners will be the same. Just be sure to position the repeat your selected way consistently.

The quilt diagrams below show several corner options. Figure 4 shows the repeats entering the corners to the outside edge of the quilt. A simple curve sweeps across the corner to connect the ends of the adjacent border repeats.

To form this, or any other corner design, first cut out a square of tracing paper exactly the size of the corner area. Fold the square in half diagonally and lightly crease to form a center guide (Figure 3). Use small pieces of tape to connect the side and end border repeats to corner square. Look carefully at Figure 3. Notice that the paper repeats are narrower than the corner square. That's because margin space had to be subtracted before the repeat was formed. If you wish, you can work with a corner square of paper whose sides are equal to the width of your repeat. I prefer using a full finished-size square, remembering as I work that the design must not run into the edge.

Figure 4

Figure 5

Figure 6

To create a corner like those in Figure 4, draw a curving line that connects the ends of the repeat lines. Remember that the line will be the center vein, so margin space will be needed to each side in order that quilted feathers will not dip into the binding area at the quilt's corners. Notice that the feathering of the corners in Figure 4 is flowing around the quilt in a clockwise direction. You might wish to review "Two Important Rules of Feathering," page 11.

The corner style of Figure 5 shows a corner that is available when the repeat enters the corner with the repeat line to the inside edge of the quilt. The plume twists around and back under itself before continuing on around the quilt in a counterclockwise direction. The procedure for forming this corner design is the same as described above for corners in Figure 4. Make a tracing paper square the finished size of the corner area. Fold it in half diagonally and lightly crease to form a center guide. Work out the center vein arrangement on paper first (Figure 6).

Figure 7 shows yet another corner option. A heart and teardrop are centered in the corner, and the feathers appear to flow out from behind this motif on each side. If you use this kind of corner, the undulating plume cannot flow continuously around the quilt. It must stop at the halfway point on each side of the quilt, be shortened slightly, and be capped with an ending semi-circle bump.

Many more corner styles, both for undulating and straight plumes, are sketched in the **Treasury** appendix. You can customize any of them just as described above for corners 4-7. You can also, of course, make up corner designs yourself. The following chapter will tell you how to transfer these designs to your quilt.

Changing Directions with Hearts and Teardrops

One of the feather variations for filling a sashing strip shown on page 16 was a straight plume with hearts at the middle, also shown in Figure 8 at right. The feathers flow to the right and the left seemingly from behind the hearts.

The practice heart you completed on page 15 also employed a small heart plus teardrop motif at the top of the design. The feathers flow out from the small heart and the teardrop in both directions to form the larger mirror-image feather heart (Figure 9).

Small hearts and teardrops are handy to use whenever you need to change the direction of a line of feathers (straight or curving). One of the corner styles discussed on pages 26 and 27 also utilizes a heart and teardrop motif to enable feathers to move out from the corner in both directions (Figure 10 at right). When working on your own feather designs, use the heart and/or teardrop to change feathering directions.

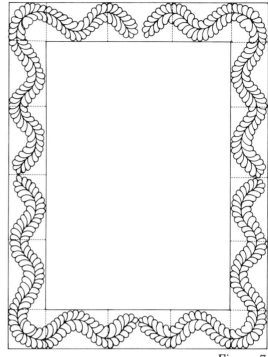

Figure 7

Figure 8

Figure 9

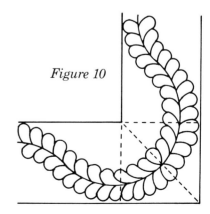

Figure 10

Feathers

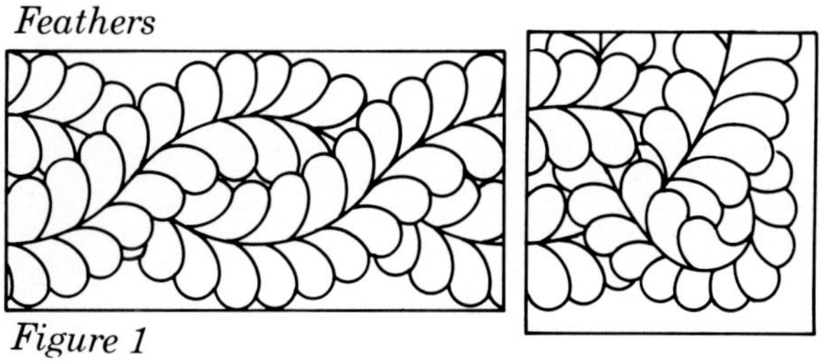

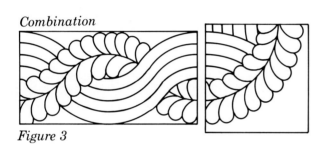

Figure 1

Cables

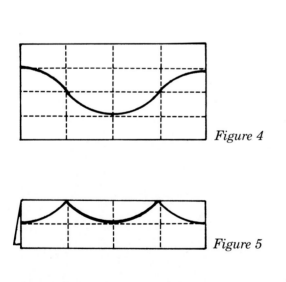

Figure 2

Combination

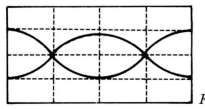

Figure 3

Interwoven Repeats

Look again at drawing exercise I on insert 2. This beautiful interwoven feather style is perfect for filling wide border areas, and is easy to create.

Once you have figured and formed the repeat for your border by folding paper as described on pages 22 and 23, fold the paper in half lengthwise and copy hill and valley lines onto all the blank planes through the middle sections of the paper (Figures 4 and 5). The resulting double repeat (Figure 6) can be used for interwoven plumes, quilted cables, or combinations, as shown in the examples opposite.

To make interwoven feathers, use a ruler to mark outer guidelines an appropriate distance from the center vein. You must arrange these lines as shown in Figure 7, so that the two plumes will appear to weave over and under as they move around the quilt. Once you have worked out this arrangement on paper, you can put as many of these units as needed end to end, regardless of whether an even or odd number, and the two plumes, or two cables, will always connect properly.

Both lines of feathering or cabling must turn the corner. Some options for corner segments are shown here.

Figure 4

Figure 5

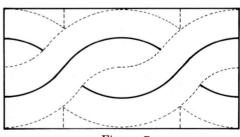

Figure 7

Figure 6

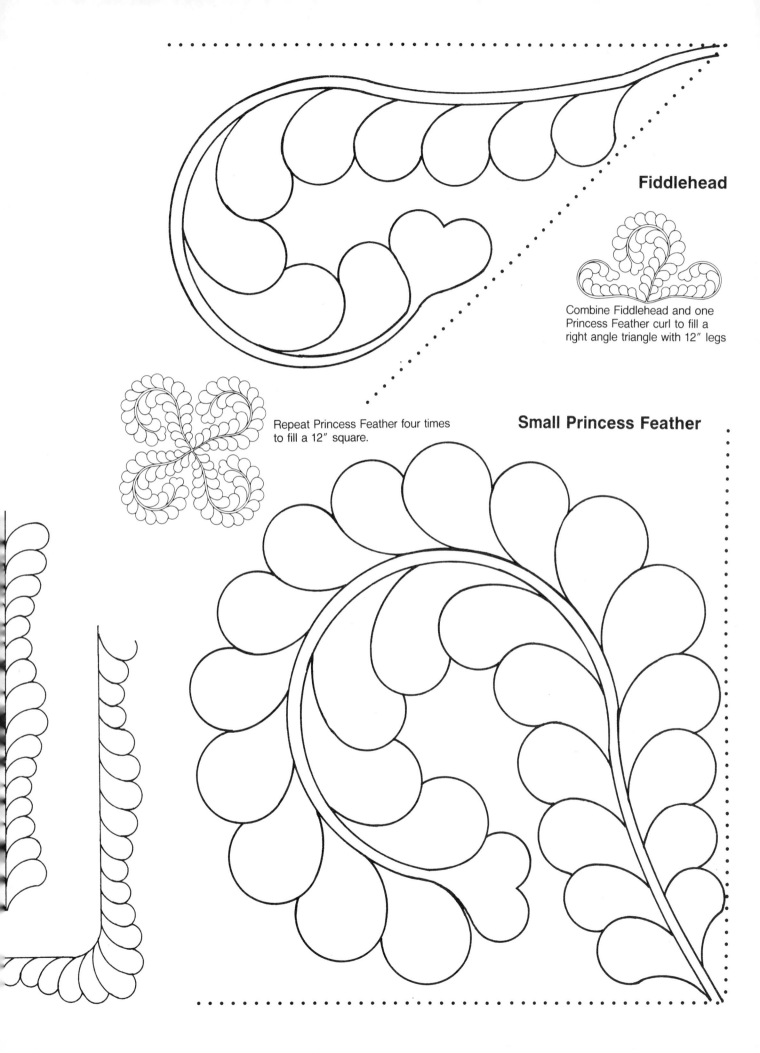

Fiddlehead

Combine Fiddlehead and one Princess Feather curl to fill a right angle triangle with 12″ legs

Repeat Princess Feather four times to fill a 12″ square.

Small Princess Feather

Kinds of Background Quilting

Square Grid

Diagonal Square Grid

Hanging Diamond

Double Diagonals

Basketweave

Teacup

Stipple

Insert # 4

Extend li
to complet

Corner Curl

Circle-in-a-Square

The corner curl fits a
setting triangle
with 6½" to 7" legs

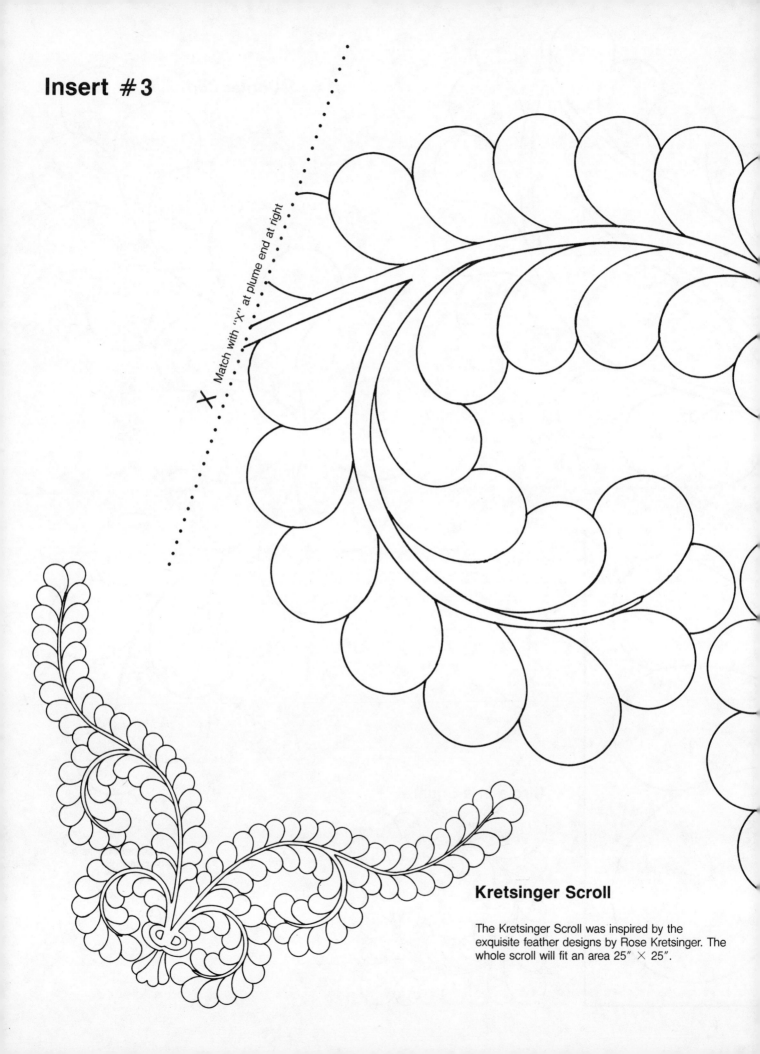

Insert #3

X Match with "X" at plume end at right

Kretsinger Scroll

The Kretsinger Scroll was inspired by the exquisite feather designs by Rose Kretsinger. The whole scroll will fit an area 25" × 25".

ne

cellaneous Motifs

Exercise F. Undulating Plume

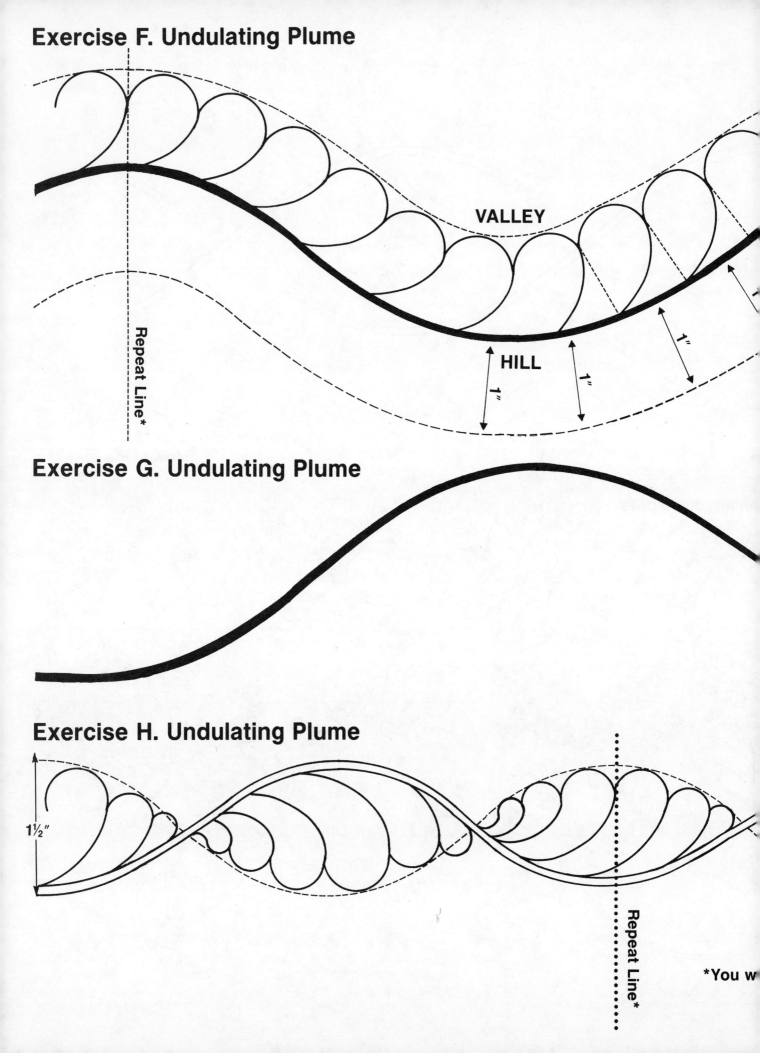

Repeat Line*

VALLEY

HILL

1"

1"

1"

Exercise G. Undulating Plume

Exercise H. Undulating Plume

1½"

Repeat Line*

*You w

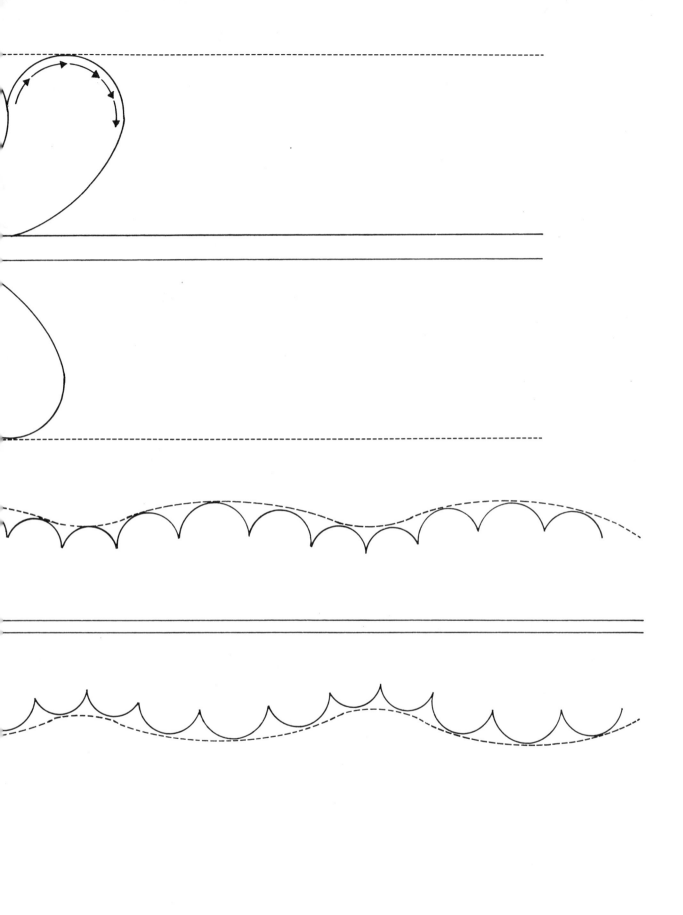

Exercise A. Straight Plume

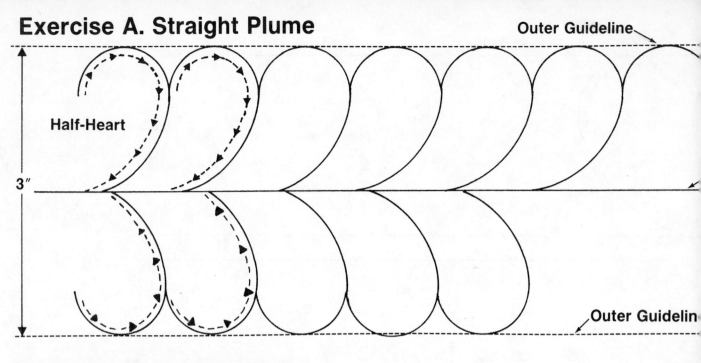

Outer Guideline

Half-Heart

3"

Outer Guidelin

Exercise B. Straight Plume

Exercise C. Straight Plume

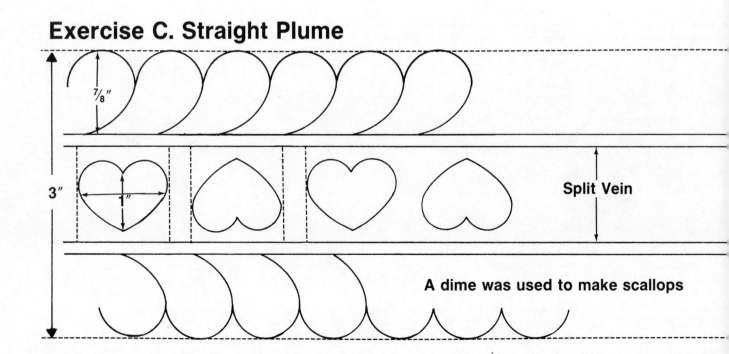

7/8"

3"

1"

Split Vein

A dime was used to make scallops

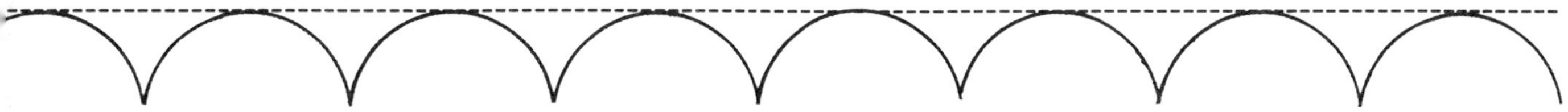

25¢ piece used as a scalloping template

ter Vein

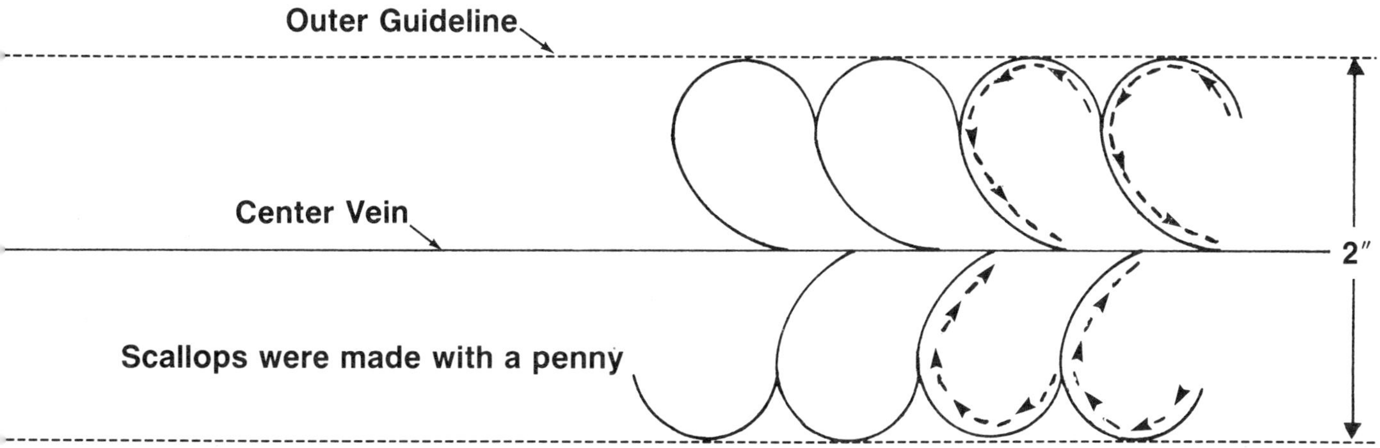

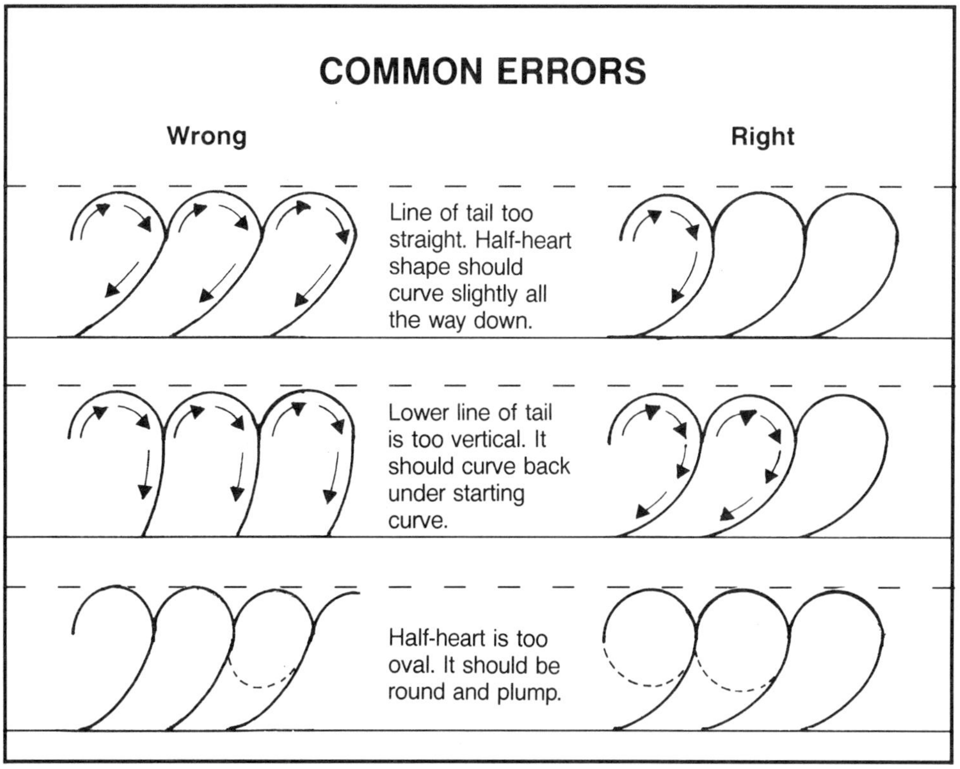

Outer Guideline

Center Vein

2"

Scallops were made with a penny

COMMON ERRORS

Wrong		Right
	Line of tail too straight. Half-heart shape should curve slightly all the way down.	
	Lower line of tail is too vertical. It should curve back under starting curve.	
	Half-heart is too oval. It should be round and plump.	

uter Guideline

Exercise D. Straight Plume

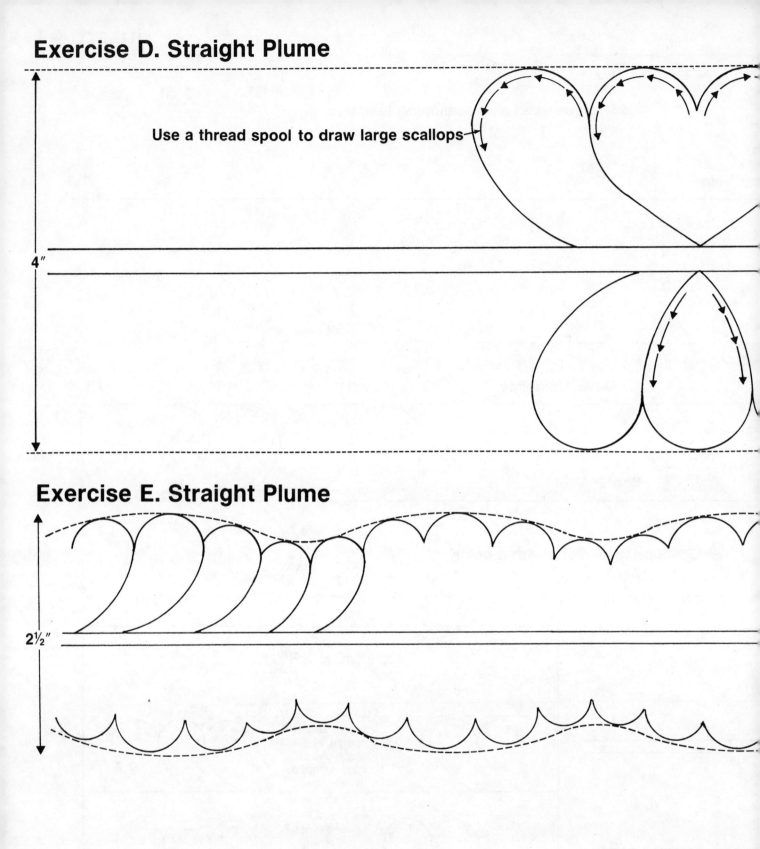

Use a thread spool to draw large scallops

4"

Exercise E. Straight Plume

2½"

HILL

VALLEY

Repeat Line*

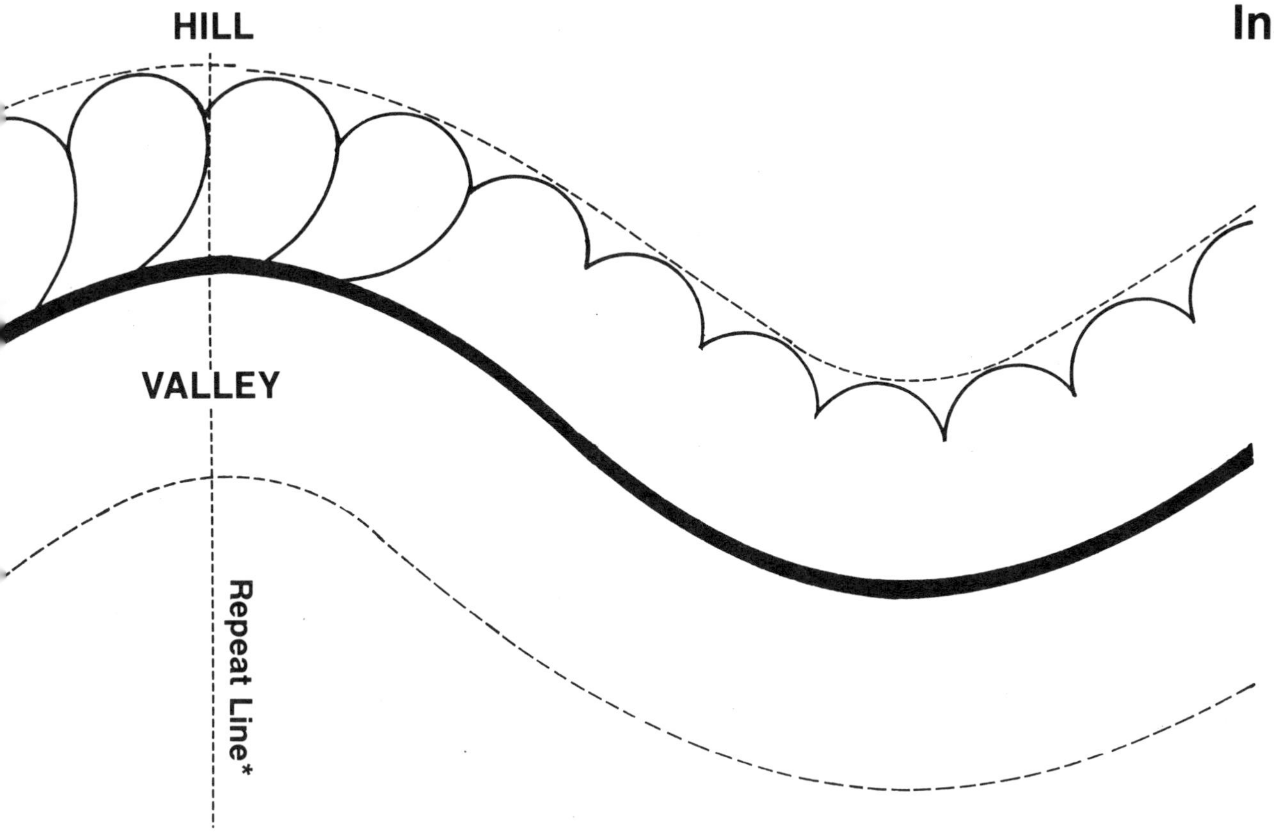

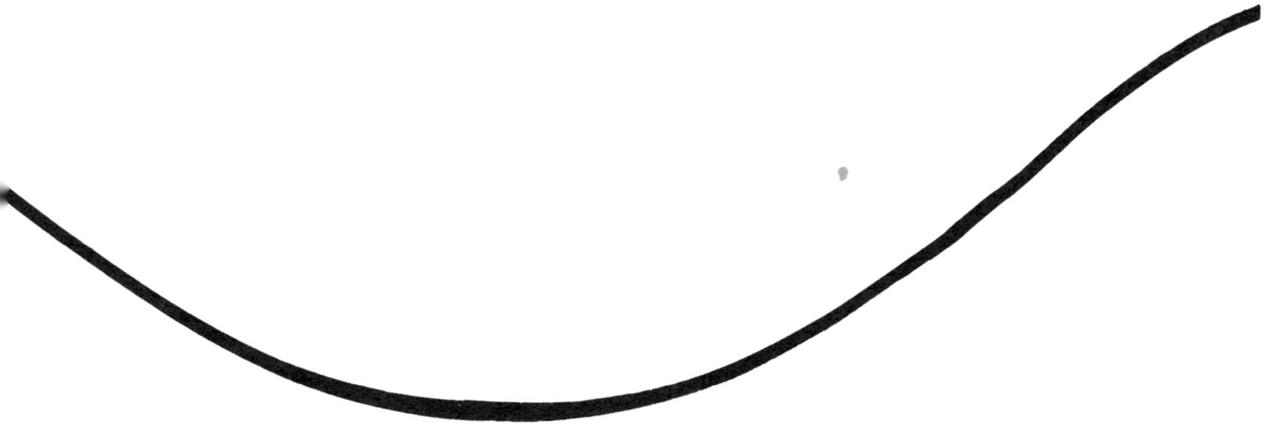

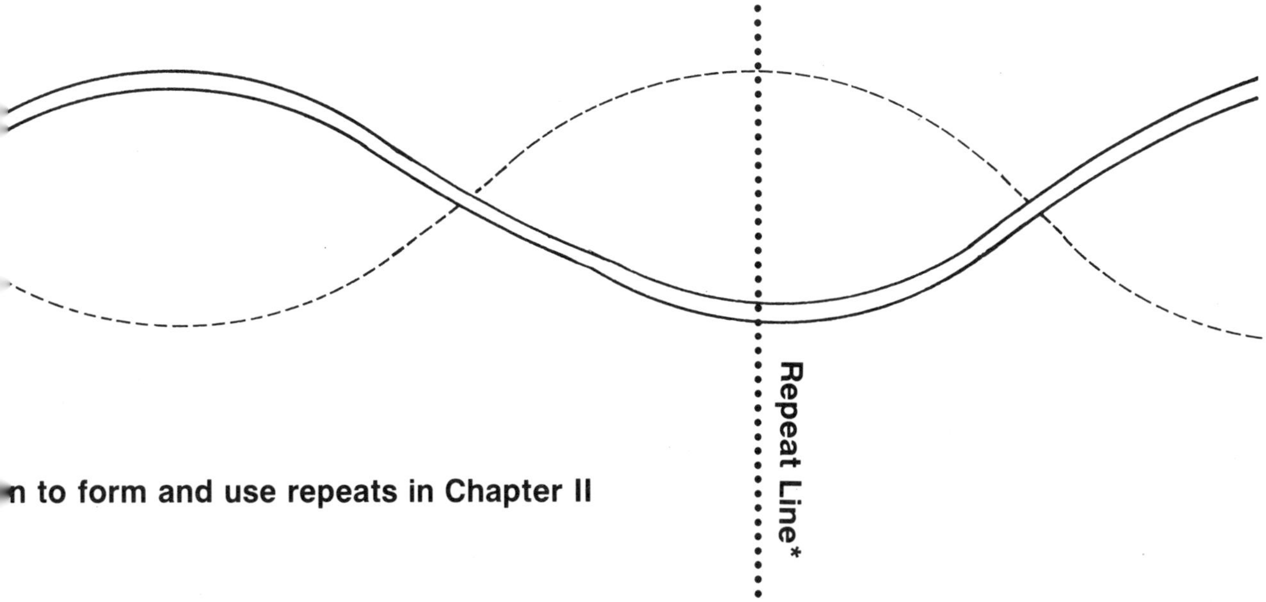

n to form and use repeats in Chapter II

Repeat Line*

Exercise I. Undulating Plume

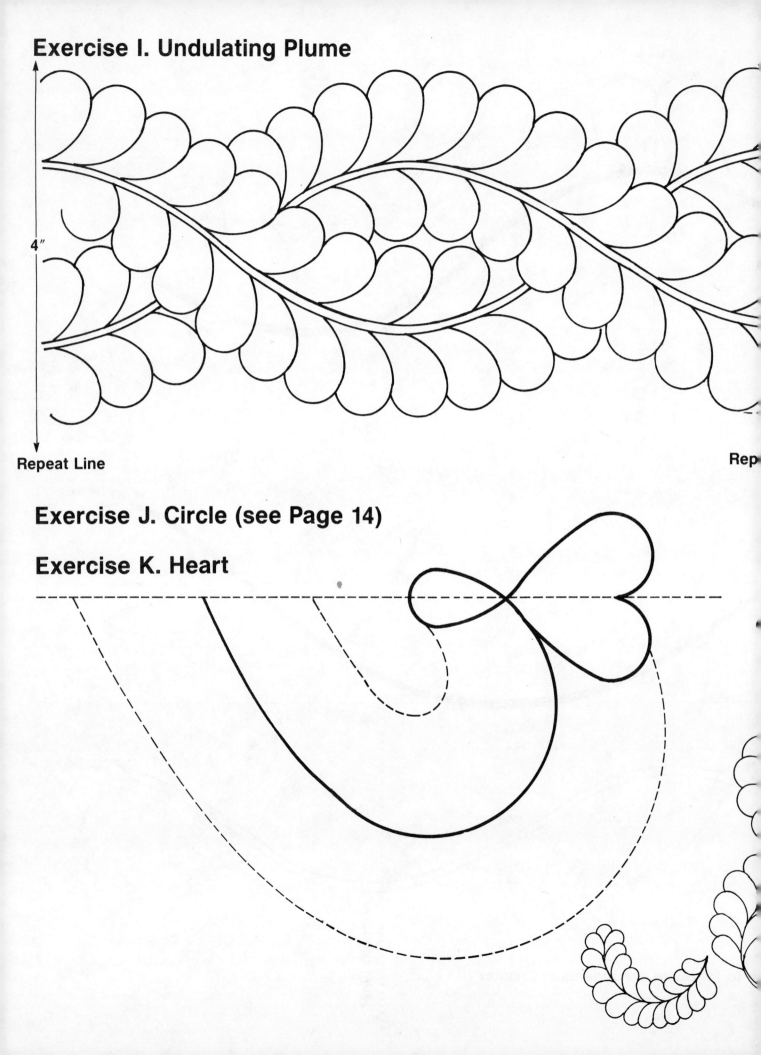

4″

Rep

Exercise J. Circle (see Page 14)

Exercise K. Heart

X Match with "X"
at plume end at left

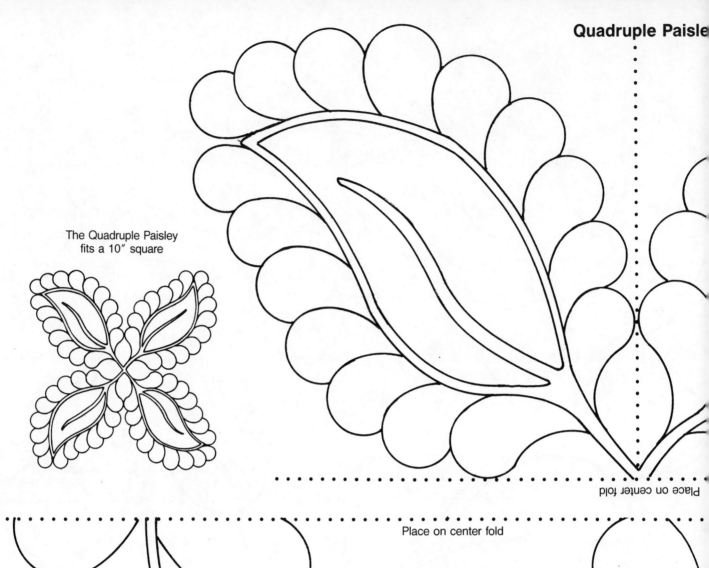

The Quadruple Paisley
fits a 10″ square

Place on center fold

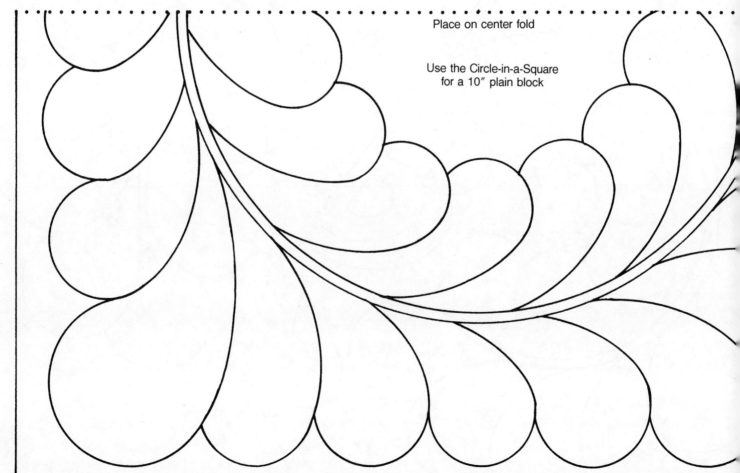

Place on center fold

Use the Circle-in-a-Square
for a 10″ plain block

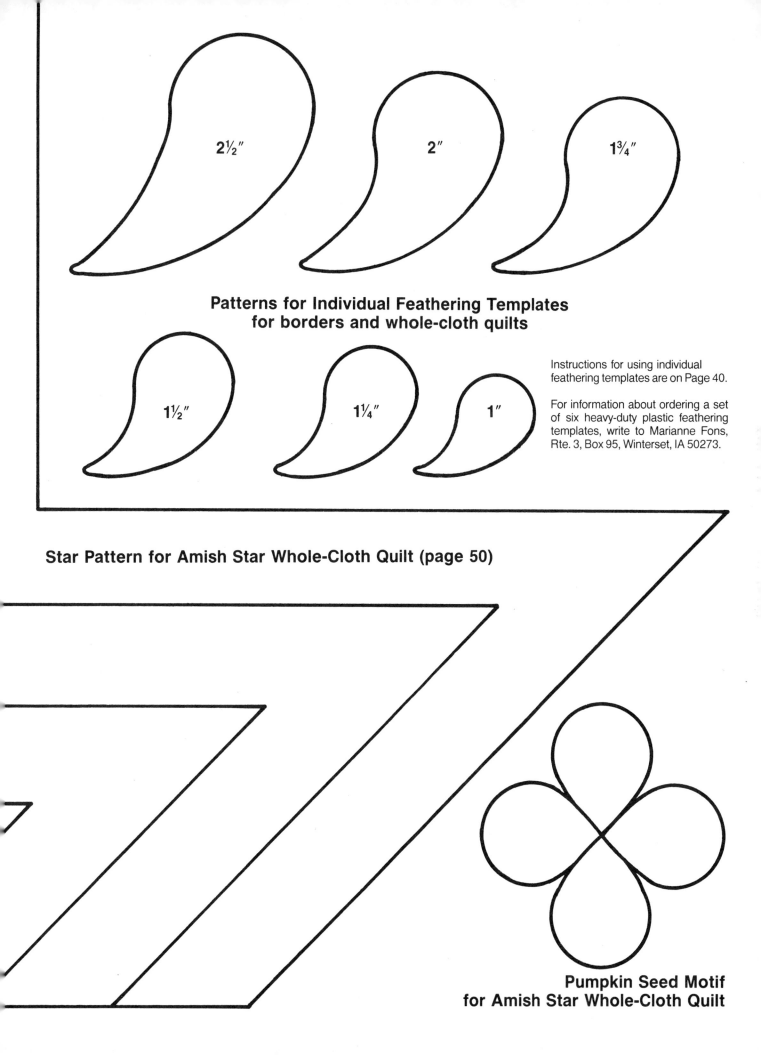

**Patterns for Individual Feathering Templates
for borders and whole-cloth quilts**

2½"

2"

1¾"

1½"

1¼"

1"

Instructions for using individual feathering templates are on Page 40.

For information about ordering a set of six heavy-duty plastic feathering templates, write to Marianne Fons, Rte. 3, Box 95, Winterset, IA 50273.

Star Pattern for Amish Star Whole-Cloth Quilt (page 50)

**Pumpkin Seed Motif
for Amish Star Whole-Cloth Quilt**

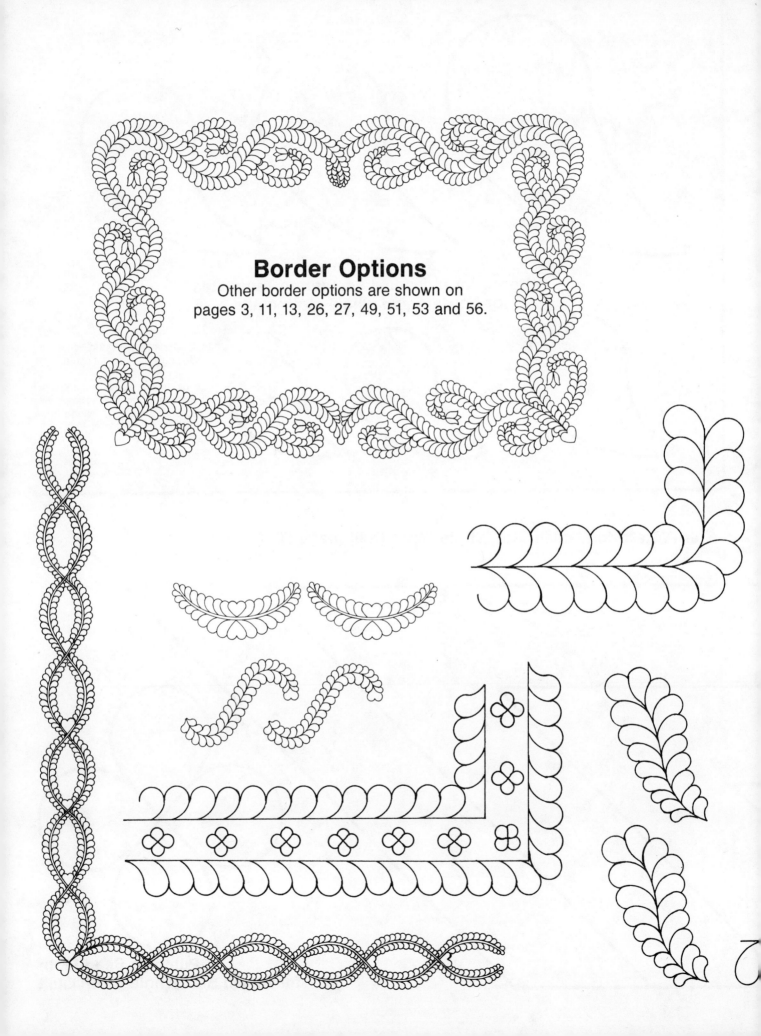

Border Options
Other border options are shown on
pages 3, 11, 13, 26, 27, 49, 51, 53 and 56.

Bonus: Repeats for Applique Vines

Study antique applique quilts and you'll see that, generally, when quilters of the past put bias vines of flowers or leaves on their borders they "winged it." You can use the techniques you've learned for figuring repeats to customize undulating quilting designs for figuring vine repeats. Your applique vines can travel smoothly all the way around a quilt with no break. The center vein now familiar to you makes a perfect winding vine.

Follow the instructions on page 22 for folding paper to form a perfect-fit repeat for your border. You will have to measure out from the center vein to arrive at placement lines for the folded edges of the bias vine because the center vein actually runs right through the middle of the border. Measure out one-half the finished width of the vine to each side of the center vein to make placement lines.

LANCASTER ROSE. Appliqued bias serves as a center vein for the feathering which beautifully compliments the flower motifs of this wall quilt. The techniques described in Chapter II for forming repeat units were modified slightly to make the undulating vine form a circle. To set off the applique and feather motifs, a 1″ diagonal grid was quilted throughout the background area. (Lancaster Rose, 40″ square, designed by Liz Porter, made by Barb Corsbie.)

LIBERTY QUILT. Repeats for undulating floral vines like the one in the outer border of Lady Liberty Medallion can be created using the techniques described in Chapter II. This quilt by Marianne Fons was the Iowa winner in the 1986 Great American Quilt Contest, sponsored by the 3M Company. The continuous vine of roses and buds was used to symbolize the growth of America's families. (Lady Liberty, 72″ square, photo courtesy 3M, Minneapolis, Minnesota.)

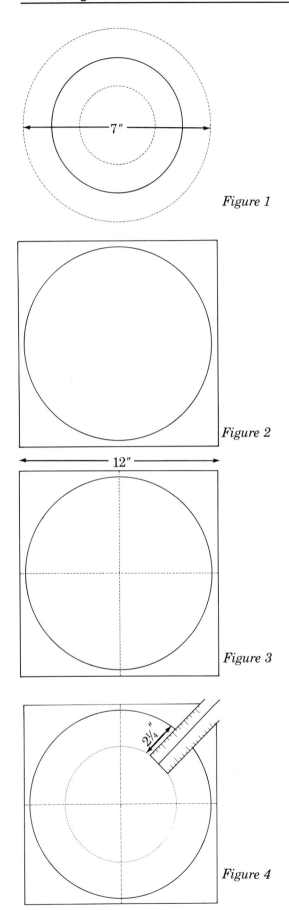

Figure 1

Figure 2

Figure 3

Figure 4

Customizing Circles and other Shapes

Circles. When you completed the exercise on page 14, you gained experience in drawing the classic feather circle or feather ring. The diameter of the outer dashed circle of that practice ring was 7″ (Figure 1). Keeping in mind that quilting designs need margins between them and seams or other design elements, the 7″ feather circle might be used to fill an 8″ - 9″ square or circular area in a quilt, giving it ½″ to 1″ margins.

To originate a feather ring for a project of your own, you must first decide on the outermost dimension of the circle. This outer guideline is always drawn first, before the center vein of the circle. If you want to use a circle in a 12″ finished square, for example, subtract ½″ to 1″ from each side of the square for margin, i.e., a 10½″ outer diameter circle would be a good size, leaving ¾″ margin at each side. The design area for the feather ring, then, is a 10½″ circle.

The next step is drawing the circle. One way to draw a circle is with an ordinary bow compass. Dime store and art store versions are two different animals. The typical inexpensive type costs a dollar or two and will make a circle up to about 12″ in diameter. Art store varieties that make up to 12″ diameters range from about $6.00 to $15.00, but they are more accurate than the dime store ones.

Available at many quilt and sewing stores is a 2″ by 18″ clear plastic ruler that has several small holes down the middle. You can put a pencil in two holes and use the ruler like a compass to draw circles from 1″ to 17″ in diameter. However, only inch-even sizes are possible. One quilters' book of grids for pattern drafting has a helpful page of perfect circles, from 1″ to 14″ in diameter, but also includes only even number diameters.

Some of the handiest tools for making circles are in your kitchen. Pot lids, bowls and plates make excellent circle templates. I often go to my kitchen, ruler in hand, to search my cupboards for the right size circle. (Digging through your utensils may remind you of all the things you used to cook before becoming a quilter!)

For very large circles, the best method is to improvise a compass with a length of string tied to a pencil. Thumbtack or hold the loose end of the string in place and draw the circle.

Use your compass or template to draw the outermost dimension of the circle on a piece of tracing paper the finished size of the square you want to fill (Figure 2). Fold the paper in half both ways, lining up the arcs, to form center guidelines as shown in Figure 3.

Now you must decide how wide you want the outer ring of feathers to be. Your decision will be based partly on the size of the circle. Naturally, a very large circle will need larger half-heart scallops than a small one. Usually, just by looking at your outer guideline circle, you can choose an appropriate width. Continuing with the example we have used already, a 10½″ diameter circle, a good width for the outer ring of feathers would be 2¼″. Using a clear plastic ruler, measure in 2¼″ all the way around the circle, making little marks as shown in Figure 4, or use your compass to draw a 6″ diameter circle within the larger one. When you connect the marks, the line you make is the center vein of the circle. If you want a double center vein, measure in another ¼″ or so, to make a slightly smaller second vein line (Figure 5).

Finally, assuming you want an inner ring of feathers, measure in one more time to form the outer guideline for that inside ring of feathers (Figure 6). Again, a compass can be used. Often, on old quilts, the inner ring is the same width as the outer one, 2¼″ in our example, but it can be narrower.

Once center vein and guidelines for your circle are established, sketch in a few scallops. Erase and redraw until the feathers seem about the right size (Figure 7). Then, if you like using a coin or spool template to make helping scallops just to the inside of the guidelines, experiment to find a coin about the size of the first feathers you sketched in. Use the coin or other template to scallop along the two guidelines. (Figure 8.) When you get back around to where you started scalloping, you may have to erase a few and "fudge" a little to make them fit.

All that remains is to draw the right and left sides of hearts to each side of the center vein. If you want your circle to flow in a clockwise direction, make right sides of hearts in the outer ring and left sides of hearts in the inner ring. For a counter-clockwise circle, draw left sides of hearts to the outside, right sides of hearts to the inside.

Remember to build the plume in the direction the feathers are flowing, (Rule # 1 on page 11). Also, recall what you learned by doing the practice circle on page 14. There will be many more feathers in the outside than in the inside ring. In the inner ring, the spaces between the tails will be wider. The tails still end basically just below the starting point of the half heart, but the extra spacing makes the half heart look extended. Once you have drawn in the feathers to your satisfaction, darken the quilting lines with a wide black permanent marker.

Study the circle variations below. More are in the **Treasury** appendix at the back of the book, where you'll also see feathered oval examples. In Chapter III you will learn how to transfer circle designs onto cloth.

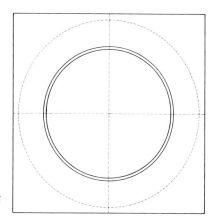

Figure 5

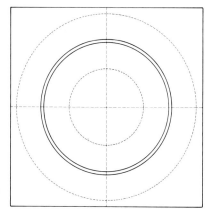

Figure 6

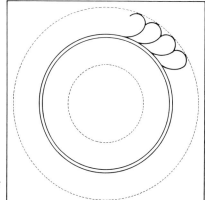

Figure 7

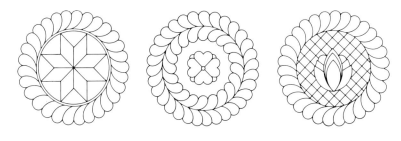

Figure 8

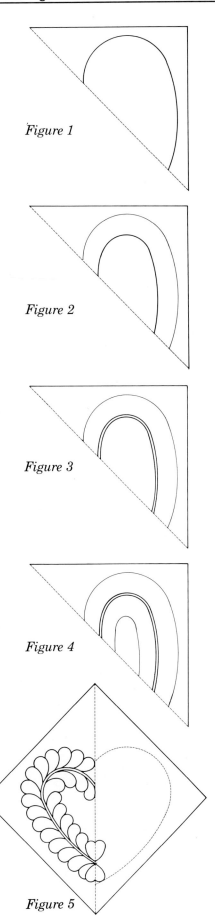

Figure 1

Figure 2

Figure 3

Figure 4

Figure 5

Hearts. Customizing heart designs is like customizing circles in that you begin by establishing the outer dimension of the heart. Let's say you want to quilt feather hearts in the setting squares of a baby quilt. The finished size of the diagonally set fabric squares is 6″.

The best way to draw any symmetrical heart, of course, is to fold a piece of paper in half, sketch half the heart on one side, and then flip the paper to trace on the other half of the heart. Customizing feather hearts works the same way. Start with a piece of tracing paper the finished size of the block, in our example, 6″ x 6″. Fold the paper in half (diagonally, since the blocks are set diagonally). Sketch one side of the heart, leaving adequate margin space (Figure 1). This line will be the outer guideline. Use a wide point black felt marker to darken the line and make it easier to trace onto the other side.

Next, use a ruler to make little marks, or sketch "by eye," a center vein, an equal distance all the way around, **inside** the outer guideline (Figure 2). In our example, ¾″ would be about right. If you want your heart to have a double vein, draw a second line (Figure 3). If you want feathers on both sides of the center vein, draw another guideline to the inside of the heart, an equal distance all the way around.

Sometimes, if you measure in to form the center vein, you may find that when you connect your small marks, the center vein heart isn't as pretty a heart shape as you'd like. Don't be afraid to erase and resketch to "plump it" a bit. As long as you pay attention to your outer guideline and remember that the feather scallops cannot trespass that line, you can play around with the inner lines.

As you should recall from the heart drawing exercise on page 15, the two sides of the heart must be mirror images, so you need only perfect one half, then trace the other side. You can work with either side. Right handed people usually find the right side easier to work with, left handed people, the left side. Work with pencil to feather both sides of the center vein. You can use a coin to form guiding scallops if you wish, or just freehand the feathers. Remember that the inner feathers, especially those in the tight upper curve of the heart, will appear elongated because their tails are more spaced out. They are still normal half-hearts. Notice how a small heart or teardrop is used effectively at the top or bottom of a feather heart to allow the feathers to travel in opposite directions on either side. In the example on this page, the feathers are running from bottom to top. The heart you did on page 15 had feathers traveling from top to bottom.

Once you have one side of the heart the way you want it, darken the lines of the feathering, fold the paper, and trace the other side to complete the design. The next chapter will show you how to transfer designs to fabric.

Other shapes. Originating feather designs for odd or irregular-shaped areas is not difficult. You simply establish the design area, draw a center vein through it, and then feather the vein so that the feathering fills the design area.

The quilted waistpockets pictured here offer good examples of "other shape" feather motifs. For a project like this, draw the full scale dimensions of the project on paper (Figure 1). Since the two sides of the pocket are mirror images, the feather design only needs to be drawn for one side and is then reversed for the other side. Sketch the outer guideline in pencil on the paper pattern (Figure 2). Draw the center vein down the middle of this design area, and add the feathers (Figure 3). The individual feather scallops get larger as the available space within the outer guidelines widens. If you are keen on using a coin as a template to make guiding scallops just inside the outer guideline, you'll need several sizes of coins to graduate the feathers like this. Once such a design is completed, darken the quilting lines so they can be traced onto fabric or template material.

The Grandmother's Fan block (Figure 4) needed quilting in the empty space at the corner. To draw a similar design, first sketch a crescent-shape outer guideline. Then draw the center vein through the middle, and fill in the feathers to each side.

Figure 5 shows how two Iowa Star blocks joined together form a fairly large area that needs quilting. To create this design, determine the outer guideline of the design area. The seam serves as a center vein. Draw graduated feathers on one side, and fold the paper to form the other, mirror-image, half. The photo on page 20 shows how nicely such a quilting pattern complements patchwork.

Many more feathering ideas are in the Treasury appendix. Adapt any of them to any size you want by using the techniques you have learned in this chapter.

WAISTPOCKETS. Women of the 19th century wore patchwork waistpockets to carry sewing supplies and other household notions. These fancier versions are fashion accessories that provide an excellent vehicle for beautiful feather quilting. The pocket on the left displays a mirror image design with feathers that grow larger as they move down to the bottom of the work. The pocket on the right has a large heart/teardrop motif at its base. The feathers travel to the top of the pocket from each side, also mirror-images. (Waistpockets, 18″ long, made by Marianne Fons.)

7½″
18″
12″

Figure 1 *Figure 2* *Figure 3*

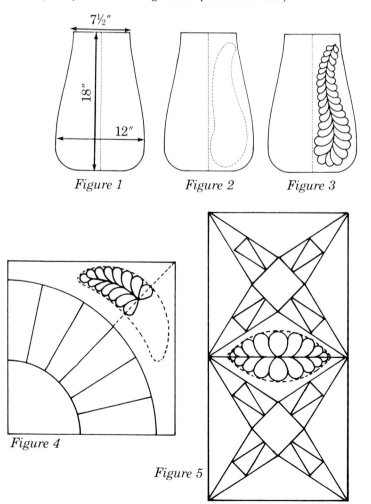

Figure 4

Figure 5

Chapter III: Marking Designs on Cloth

"On every point of technique there is a difference of opinion, but quilters are inclined to be more dogmatic about the (quilting) patterns and how they are marked than about any other point in their craft."

Mavis Fitzrandolph,
Traditional Quilting, 1954

Getting quilting designs on quilt tops has always been a problem step in the quiltmaking process. The marks must be dark enough to see for quilting, but must also be light enough or removable so they don't detract from the quilt once it's finished. A further complication is the fact that light and dark fabrics, and all the values of prints and solids in between, are used in quilt tops. A single marking technique won't work for all quilts, or even all the fabrics in one quilt.

Marking Tools

Quilters of the past naturally marked with tools and materials that were close at hand. A technique which is rarely practiced now is needle marking, widely used in England around the turn of the century. According to Mavis Fitzrandolph in **Traditional Quilting** (1954), a large, not-too-sharp needle was used to "draw" on the quilt top surface. Called "scratching," this method involves pressing the quilting design into the fabric, usually by drawing against a hard template with the needle held at a sharp angle. Templates in the north of England were cut from wood, tin or stiff cardboard. Fitzrandolph's fascinating book, no longer in print, includes photographs of a County Durham quilter marking feathers in this fashion, using a penny as a template.

Needle marking is also described in **Quilts in America** (1974) by Patsy and Myron Orlofsky (pages 138-139). They state that scratching was often used for masterpiece quilts that would never be washed. Indeed, my friend Liz Porter recalls her grandmother marking quilting in this manner, but only on her "fancy quilts."

My own experimentation with this technique has found it a usable method if your eyesight is extremely good. Though the indentations are hard to see and only a small portion of the quilting can be marked at a time, the problem of removing marks after quilting is completely eliminated.

Another old time marking method was called "pouncing." Small holes were punched along the design lines of a paper or cardboard pattern by hand with a needle or with an unthreaded sewing machine. Powdered cinnamon or charcoal (for light fabrics) or chalk, cornstarch or flour (for dark fabrics) was dusted through the holes in the pattern, which was pinned or otherwise fixed to the quilt surface. Though such powders do wash out, they also tend to disappear too soon. If the quilting is done in a frame, the powder rubs onto the sleeves of the quilter. Such markings would probably not last any length of time on a quilt being quilted in a hoop. The marking would have to be done as the quilting progressed.

Quiltmaker Michael James, in **The Quiltmakers Handbook** (1978), describes a variation of the pounce method in his section on quilting. He advocates lightly penciling over the powdered design after the perforated pattern is removed. James also describes perforating patterns, either purchased or original ones, by using an unthreaded sewing machine to "stitch" along the lines, or by making holes with a pin or nail. James also describes a technique using a dressmaker's wheel and tracing carbon.

Quilters have also traditionally used slivers of soap, light or dark, to mark quilting lines. There is no problem in washing these marks out of course, but they also tend to rub off during the quilting and work best if marking can be done a little at a time. One quilter has speculated that some soaps, especially "modern" ones containing chemicals, might damage fabrics if left in too long.

Several kinds of pens and pencils are currently in use for marking designs on quilt tops. Artist's pencils, available in art and office supply stores, and at quilt shops, will mark many fabrics and will keep a fine point so that a thin quilting line can be drawn. White and silver pencils are the most popular. The silver will show on most light or dark fabrics. These pencils make marks that last well through the quilting. The quilting stitches themselves cover most of the thin marked line, and the rest seems to rub away as the quilting is done. On many fabrics, the marks launder out. Other color pencils can also be used — select a color only slightly different from the fabric being marked.

A good lead pencil for light fabrics is a mechanical pencil with hard (# 3), thin (0.5) leads. No sharpening is required to keep a fine point, since the lead is pushed out when you press the end of the pencil. Lead pencil marks do not always wash out, so care must be taken in marking. The lines must be so thin they can be covered by the quilting thread. Some quilt shops sell a type of eraser that will remove lightly drawn pencil marks.

Another currently available tool is a soapstone marker that consists of a soapstone "lead" in a metal holder. This lead must be sharpened often during marking to maintain a fine point, but it does show up well on dark fabrics. The marks stay on reasonably well during quilting and do wash out. Many quilters advocate this tool.

Controversial marking tools introduced in the late 1970s are the washable marking pens and pencils. The pens resemble felt-tip pens and make light blue, or sometimes purple, marks that are very easy to see on light and some dark fabrics. One variety of purple pen has ink that disappears automatically within twenty-four hours. It's designed for temporarily marking buttonholes or hems, not quilting designs! The pencil versions have colored leads and can be sharpened. Cold water, dabbed or sprayed on the marks after quilting, removes them. A distinct advantage of marking with this type of tool is that errors in marking can be removed. Many quilters express concern, however, that these chemical markings do not wash out completely, but are only trapped in the batting, and can resurface later and damage the quilt. Others tell horror stories about the blue marks becoming brown and permanent when exposed to heat. I have used the pen type wash-out marker a great deal with no disasters, but I only use it on projects I am willing to machine wash once they are quilted and bound. I feel that immersion and agitation of the entire project in a large amount of cold water (no soap) rinses the chemicals out completely.

A new quilt marking product of the 1980s is a chalk wheel. A small flat reservoir holds white or colored chalk. A serrated wheel at the bottom deposits a thin chalk line on the cloth as the tool is rolled along the surface.

Another new tool designed for making quilting design stencils is an electric stencil cutting pen, sold in quilt shops and by several mail order suppliers. The quilt design is drawn on thin plastic. Then the hot stylus of the electric pen is used to burn holes or slots through the plastic at intervals along the design line. Bridges must be left between portions of the quilting line to keep the stencil intact. After removing the stencil from the quilt top surface, the quilting lines are completed free hand.

Writer and quiltmaker Louise Townsend in a February 1987 article in **Quilter's Newsletter Magazine,** describes a technique that involves cutting portions of the quilting design from peel-off sticky-back vinyl paper. These "templates" are stuck lightly to the quilt surface and quilting is done right next to their edge. The advantage of such a technique, of course, is that no marks whatsoever are put on the quilt surface. An application of this method for feather designs will be described below, in the section on "Marking Feather Borders," Paragraph B.

One other new wrinkle in the quilt marking department is a transfer fabric that resembles the stuff sold in fabric stores for tracing off garment patterns. Because the thin synthetic material is transparent, any quilting design can be traced right onto it. Then the marked pattern material is pinned to the quilt top. The lines on the porous pattern material can be gone over with most any marking pen or pencil and the marks go through onto the cloth. After the design is marked on one area of the top, it can be re-pinned on a different area.

Test First!

Before using any of these or other marking methods, a test should be made to make sure the marks will come out. The marking instrument should be tried out on a scrap of the fabric from the quilt and then washed. This is boring to do; when most quiltmakers finish a top, they are eager to get on with quilting, not marking tests. However, if you use a marking technique or tool without testing it first, and the marks don't come out, you have only yourself to blame.

TREE OF LIFE QUILT. The changing colors in the setting triangles of this Tree of Life quilt represent the changing seasons of the year, beginning with the cold blues of winter at the top and moving down to the harvest hues of autumn. Feather rings in the setting pieces and an undulating feather border soften the hard edges of the patchwork blocks. The quartered setting squares illustrate how much better quilting shows up on lighter value fabrics than darker ones. Instructions for drawing a feather circle any size are in Chapter II. (Tree of Life, 69″ x 86″, made by Marianne Fons.)

ALL QUILTED VEST. Small feather sprays are easy to draw, and make attractive motifs for garments such as this all-over quilted vest. The feather design on the vest back is repeated four times to form a ring-like central motif that encloses four tulips. A ½″ grid within the feather sprays enlarges to 1″ beyond them. A shortened version of the feather spray was used with two tulips on the vest front. (Vest by Marianne Fons, using a garment pattern by Lesly-Claire Greenberg.)

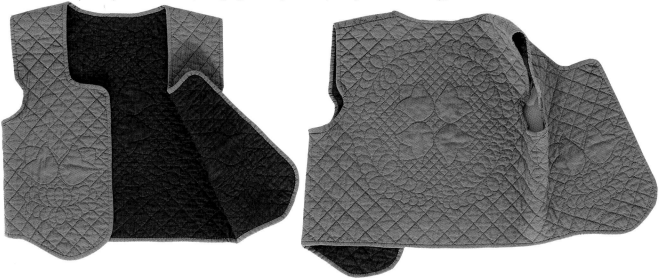

Mark Before, or After Basting?

As usual, quilters disagree on whether a quilt top should be marked before or after it is basted, but I personally advocate marking a quilt before layering it with batting and backing. For me, marking the top with it laid flat on   a hard surface helps the cloth take a thin mark better than if there is cushioney padding underneath. Also, a sharp marking pencil can poke a hole in a basted quilt top. However, I have often marked the individual feather scallops of an undulating plume border **after** basting. I mark only the center vein with the quilt flat on a table and then add the individual feathers later as I quilt, as described in Paragraph B in the "Marking Feather Borders" section below, just to avoid the tedium of marking all the feather scallops at once. I don't recommend this type of marking-as-you-go for the feathers of a whole-cloth quilt, however. It should be completely marked before basting. Full instructions for whole-cloth quilts are in Chapter V.

Quilting Pattern Under the Quilt, or Template Over It?

The methods available for marking your quilt depend on whether your fabric is light enough that the pattern can be laid under the quilt and traced onto its surface or whether your fabric is so dark you must make some sort of template and mark from the top. Positioning patterns under the quilt top makes for the easiest marking.

Under the quilt. Very light fabrics allow a design that is drawn on paper to be traced easily. As you have learned in your study of feather designs thus far, any feather design has to be worked out on paper first anyway. Most medium to medium-dark fabrics can also be traced through when taped to a window or laid on a light box. Working with small projects at a window is fairly easy, but a full size quilt is impossible to tape to vertical glass! However, a large quilt top can be spread over a glass topped coffee table or other improvised light box, and positioned as needed over the quilting design.

The feather motif used for the setting squares of the Ocean Waves quilt shown on page 17, was first worked out on tracing paper. Then the square of paper, with darkened design lines, was glued to a square of template plastic the exact

Figure 1

Figure 2

Figure 3

Figure 4

Figure 5

finished size of the fabric square to strengthen the pattern and make it easy to position. The plastic square was lightly taped to the surface of a glass-topped table and the quilt top was shifted around over the design until all the squares were marked. The waistpockets pictured on page 33 were also marked with the pattern underneath the fabric. The design was achieved as described on page 33 and then taped to a window and simply traced onto the light colored cloth. One way to improvise a light table is to lay a piece of glass or clear plastic across the seats of two chairs facing each other. In the daytime, enough light may naturally come through, or a small lamp can be placed on the floor under the glass.

Over the Quilt. Difficult-to-mark fabrics have to be marked from the top. Such fabrics can be problematic in two ways. They may be difficult because they are too dark to be traced through easily, or because none of the marks made by the available marking tools show up well on them. This second type of problem fabric is usually a print. I invariably purchase a print because I like the color or design. I never think about potential marking problems when I'm in a fabric store, or even when I am at home selecting fabrics for a particular project. Thus I have sewn fabrics into a quilt that were real headaches to mark.

Many of the prints in the Tree of Life quilt (page 36) fell into this category, especially one of the green prints used in the setting triangles of the third row. The fabric is dark green with all-over white vines. Neither light nor dark marks showed up very well, so a combination of washable marking pen and white artist's pencil was used, marking from the top with a plastic template. The print used in the background of the blocks and in the wide print border was also of this difficult print type. I used washable marking pen, marked the feathers as I quilted, and machine washed the quilt when it was finished.

Templates for Feather Motifs on Difficult Fabrics

Once you have worked out a feather design on paper, you can make a template to use for marking it on your quilt top. Let's say you have customized a feather cross (Figure 1) for a portion of your project. Glue your paper design on cardboard or template plastic and then cut out, on the outer edge, the three portions of the design you need (Figure 2).

Before marking, make light crease lines, just by finger pressing, vertically, horizontally and diagonally on the fabric.

Trace around the portions of the design using the crease lines as guidelines. Carefully draw the center vein through the middle and complete the individual feather scallops.

Feathering templates for a heart and for a circle with a double vein would look like Figures 3-5. Of the templates illustrated for the heart (Figures 3,4), the small one is for the inner feathers and the larger template is for the outer ones. The smaller template would fit exactly inside the larger one because the heart has just a single center vein. The two feather circle templates (Figure 5) have a narrow space between them so that the circle will have a double center vein. Marking with these templates gives you the center vein and outer bumps of each side of the design. After marking around and removing these templates from the fabric surface, you have to freehand the tail of each feather.

Marking a Double Feather Circle on a Dark Fabric

1. Draw around the inner and outer edges of the plastic template for the outer ring of the feather circle to create one side of the double center vein and the "humps" of the feathers in the outer ring.
2. Remove the template and complete the tails of each feather of the outer ring.
3. Use the smaller template to mark the remaining line of the double center vein and the humps of the inner feathers. Complete the tails of the individual feathers.
4. Use a ruler to mark any desired grid quilting after feather motifs are marked.

Marking Feather Borders

In Chapter II, you learned how to customize border repeats for undulating plumes. Border plumes require hundreds of individual feather scallops. Although the distinction has been made above regarding marking with the pattern **under** or **over** the quilt top, a combination method can be used to ease the tedium of marking all those feathers in continuous borders. It involves marking just the center vein, with pattern below, and then using an individual feather template to add the feathers, even on light fabrics.

Once you have figured and formed your repeat as described on page 22, thicken the repeat line on the paper with a heavy black marker if you want a double vein. Add outer guidelines and feather the two sides of the center vein as shown in Figure 6. Think about how you want the repeat positioned on your border. Notice how in Figure 7 the side border uses an odd number of repeats. One repeat must be placed on the border with its middle aligned with the middle of the border and the "hill" to the inner edge of the border.

The end borders use an even number of repeats. The side and end repeats must always be positioned the same way, so the repeats for the end borders in Figure 7 are also placed with the hill to the inner quilt. Before you can mark any undulating border, you must decide how you want to place the repeat in the border and what kind of corner you want. (You may wish to review "A Few Words About Placing Repeats in Borders," page 23.)

A. Light Fabrics. If your fabric is light enough to trace through, you can lay the tracing paper repeat under your fabric and trace the center vein on the cloth. Remember that your repeat is slightly narrower than your fabric border so that the plumes will have margin to each side. Be sure to position the paper repeat in the middle of the border, or, you can glue the tracing paper repeat to another piece of paper that is exactly the width of the fabric repeat. For a double center vein, draw to each side of the thickened repeat line.

You'll also need to make a pattern for your corner design. Corner options are discussed on page 26. Position the repeat under each section of the border and draw only the center vein. Don't add the feathers yet. Of course if your quilt is a rectangle, you may have two different repeats as well as the corner center vein to mark.

Figure 6

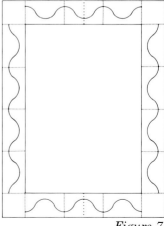

Figure 7

Figure 8

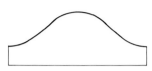

Figure 9

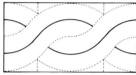

Figure 10

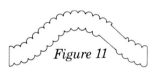

Figure 11

Figure 12

B. Individual Feather Templates. Once the center vein is marked on the entire border, take a look at the feathers you have drawn on the tracing paper repeat. Of those in the "valley" area, choose the one that you think looks nicest. Darken its outline so you can see it easily to trace it onto template plastic. Or, you can glue the individual feather shape onto cardboard. Cut out the template. This template, because it was made from a feather scallop in the area where extra spacing occurs between the feathers, will be shaped more like a comma than a true half-heart (Figure 8). This individual feather template can be used to draw feathers on both sides of the marked center vein in your border.

Marking with an individual feather template becomes easy with just a little practice. Hold the template on the fabric with your index finger. The tail portion should curve gently into the center vein. Mark around the template starting at the beginning of the hump each time. As you move along the hills and valleys, you will need to adjust the small template, allowing the tail portion to cross over the center vein as needed to space the feathers attractively and keep the whole border plume a consistent width. You will flip the template over to reverse the scallop shape for the opposite side of the vein and make right sides of hearts on one side and left sides of hearts on the other. Draw the plume to run either clockwise or counterclockwise.

Templates can also be made of peel-off sticky back paper advocated by Louise Townsend and previously described under "Marking Tools." You can make a number of left and right templates, stick them next to the center vein and quilt just at the edge. Patterns for several handy sizes of individual feather templates are given in the **Treasury** appendix.

C. Difficult Fabrics. If the fabric of your border is one of those "difficult" ones you can't trace through, you'll have to make a center vein template and mark it on the border from the top.

Glue your drawn tracing paper repeat onto thin template plastic. Make the template plastic the full finished-size width of the fabric border. If you want a double vein, thicken the repeat line. Cut the plastic to form a repeat template that looks like Figure 9. Place this template on the border and mark the center vein all the way around the quilt. (Of course if your quilt is a rectangle, you may have to make a center vein template for each of two different repeats.)

You'll also need to make a template for your corner design. Since you will use the corner template only four times, you could cut and use your paper corner if you want.

Make an individual feather template as described in section B above and use it as described to feather both sides of the center vein all the way around the quilt.

Marking an Undulating Border on a Dark Fabric

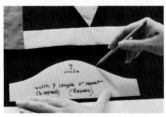

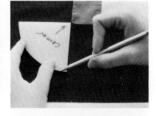

1. Use repeat template to mark center vein in the border. If the quilt is a rectangle, you will have a different repeat for side and end borders.

2. Marking with a corner template connects the center veins marked on borders.

3. Use an individual feather template to mark the feathers along the center vein. Flip the small template to reverse the half-heart shape from side to side on the center vein.

D. Baste the Quilt. If you wish, you can go ahead and layer and baste the quilt top, batting and backing once the center vein is marked. Then, if you quilt in a hoop, you can move the hoop along the border, using the individual feather template to feather the portion of the center vein in the hoop as you go. If you use a frame, you can also just feather a portion of the border at a time.

Interwoven Borders

If your interwoven border is going on a fabric you can trace through, prepare your tracing paper repeat so that it looks like Figure 10. Lay it under the border. Draw on the center vein and trace in the feathers or use an individual feather template to feather each repeat section as you go. If your double feather design is for a fabric you can't see through at all, trace the paper repeat to make two identical templates like the one shown in Figure 11. Use one with the hill to the inside of the quilt and one with the hill to the outside. Pay close attention to the over-under arrangement. After you have the outer scallops drawn on the fabric, you can cut the templates down the middle (Figure 12) and use them to add the center veins. Complete the feathers by drawing the tails down from the outer scallops smoothly into the center vein.

Don't Forget About Straight Lines

Many feather quilting designs are greatly enhanced by grids or other straight line background quilting. A ruler is the most common template, of course, used for marking lines. Some quilters use different widths of masking tape as guides for straight-line quilting. An excellent aid for marking an inch-even grid on cloth you can trace through is a large fold-out cardboard sewing/cutting board, sold in most fabric stores. These 30″ x 60″ boards are available with a 1″ grid printed on them. The grid can be positioned under fabric and the straight lines traced onto the fabric using a ruler.

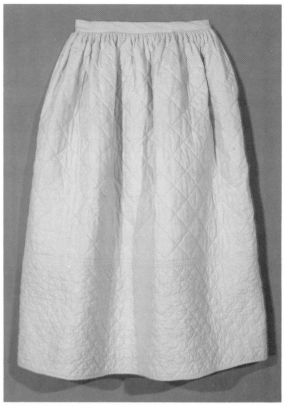

QUILTED SKIRT. Quilted petticoats or underskirts date back to the Renaissance, and were popular in some form through the 19th century. Historians speculate that American quiltmaking may have its origins in such "whole-cloth" items. This modern example has a lower border of interwoven feather plumes backed by a 1″ grid. The upper skirt is quilted in a 2″ diagonal grid. (Quilted skirt, 36″ long, made by Marianne Fons, using a garment pattern by Folkwear.)

PRINCESS FEATHER DETAIL. The techniques described for forming simple border repeats can also be used to create interwoven feather plumes, cables, or combinations like this feather/cable border that fills a 9″ wide section of the Princess Feather whole-cloth quilt.

Chapter IV: How to Quilt Feathers

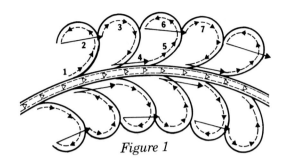

Figure 1

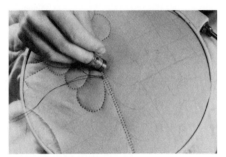

Photo 1

Photo 2

Photo 3

Photo 4

Every quilter likes to get the most out of her length of quilting thread. Most quilters agree that the first stitch is the hardest, so the fewer numbers of knottings and startings the better. Books, and my early quilting teachers, recommended using fairly short lengths of thread when quilting, presumably so the thread won't wear out being drawn so many times through the cloth. This has always made good sense to me, and I have generally passed the advice on to my own students. The truth is, however, when I'm quilting, especially feathers, I cut off a piece of thread as long as my arm. I've learned to quilt faster over the years, and feather patterns use up thread rapidly.

I quilt my feathers as diagrammed in Figure 1, quilting the center vein first and then the feathers, slipping through the batting with my needle from one to another until I run out of thread. I believe these "bridges" of thread hidden within the batting are preferable to knots. If a person sits or pulls on a quilt that has bridges, the threads seem to me more likely to give, whereas knots would be likely to pop through the top. Of course, my quilts have plenty of knots hidden in the batting, too.

I quilt in a hoop, and I always have several threads going at once so I can quilt every part of the design that's in the hoop before moving it to another area. I just use one needle, though, because needles fixed in the quilt get in the way when I move my hoop, and because I'm afraid of losing needles in the rug.

The trick of "travelling" by turning the needle, point to eye, through the hole in the cloth to move distances through the batting, was shown me by the exquisite quilters of the Clarksville, Tennessee area. I had already quilted thousands of feathers, but "Tennessee travelling" had never occurred to me! I had long been slipping from one quilting point to another through the batting, but when my needle was too short to make a reach, I would bring the needle and thread out halfway across, then go back into the batting through the hole I made. Sometimes I would accidentally catch a single thread, making a tiny undesirable dimple in the quilt top.

To "travel," run your needle through the batting as far as its length. Stick the point of the needle out through the fabric (Photo 1). Grasp the point of the needle (Photo 2), but don't pull it all the way out of the work as you normally would. Just hold the point and pivot the needle around (Photo 3) until you have the eye positioned at the place you want to quilt next. Push the eye through the fabric (Photo 4) and then, grasping the still-threaded eye, pull the needle and thread out of the work and begin quilting the next feather hump.

With the Tennessee quilters' method, you can move around through the batting anywhere you want, just by pivoting the needle, point to eye and eye to point, without ever making a dimple. However, using this technique may affect the truth when you say there are two spools of thread in your quilt!

Chapter V: The Whole-Cloth Quilt

Now that you've mastered feathering and customizing feather designs, you might feel ambitious enough to tackle a major project: a whole-cloth quilt. Instructions for my own way of executing the whole-cloth quilt are given in this chapter. It involves using two lengths of 44″ wide fabric for each side of the quilt, and, of course, working the designs out on paper first. The large fabric top is sectioned off preliminary to marking, simply to get all those yards of cloth under control.

Three medallion-style whole-cloth designs are given in this chapter. Notice that all three of the whole-cloth designs given here have a large central main motif. The biggest pitfall in designing a whole-cloth quilt is using a too-small pattern at the center. The central motif must carry the design weight of the whole quilt, so it must make an important design statement. Think in terms of making the main motif almost large enough to cover the mattress top.

Don't be afraid to design your own whole-cloth masterpiece, though, by combining motifs from the **Treasury** appendix, studying pictures of antique whole-cloth works, or originating your own motifs.

How to Make a Whole-Cloth Quilt
Fabric, Thread and Marking Tools:
Fabric requirements for a full size quilt: 6 yards of two solid (not print) fabrics, 100% cotton (44″-45″ wide), plus ½ to 1 yard fabric for binding.
Other Supplies (usually found at sewing supply stores):
36″ x 60″ cardboard sewing/cutting board ruled with a 1″ grid
24″ or other clear plastic ruler
Marking instruments (see Chapter III)
Paper for making large patterns
Wide tip permanent black marking pen

Fabric. The white work quilts were, of course, made of all-white cloth. You can make your whole-cloth quilt bleached or unbleached muslin on both sides if you want, or you can choose from the many beautiful solid color all-cottons currently available. Some quilt supply shops sell 80″ or 90″ wide 100% cotton muslin for quilt backs. If you used this fabric, you could have a true whole-cloth quilt with no seams. Often, however, the quality of this wide fabric is not as good as narrower yardage. Some quilters have used bed sheets for quilt backings or whole cloth quilts. However, all-cotton ones are rare, and the weave is usally too dense for easy needling.

My whole-cloth pictured on Page 25 was made of two shades of lavendar, bound with the darker shade. There are two seams on the top. Whatever colors you choose, I encourage you to make at least one of them a shade light enough so that you can trace your designs on with the pattern laid underneath the fabric. Keep in mind, too, that quilting shows up best on light fabrics. If you really want to have both sides very dark, you will have to make templates as described in Chapter III and mark the fabric from the top. Note that a light shade of fabric does not mean light weight, thin fabric. I am referring to a light color, a pastel.

Use only the very best quality cotton broadcloth for your whole cloth quilt. Keep in mind also that fabrics sold as 44″-45″ wide are sometimes narrower than that, and can become even narrower after prewashing. Some width is also lost when the panels are sewn together as described below.

Quilting Thread. Since you will be marking the lighter of the two fabrics, and therefore quilting from that side, you may want to match your quilting thread to the darker, underneath color. Although a quilter's goal is to have stitches the same on both sides, most quilters make their best stitches on the side on which they quilt. By quilting with the darker thread, the strongest thread/fabric contrast will be on the side you can most easily judge and control as you quilt. Matching the thread to the underneath side will camouflage any inconsistencies there.

Marking Tools. If you use some type of washable marker, any mistakes you make during the marking will be removeable. I used the pen-type washable marker to mark my whole-cloth quilt, machine washing the entire project upon completion (in cold water, without soap). If you use lead pencil to mark, the marks may not wash out, so you must be extra careful not to make any mistakes. Review Chapter III regarding the available types of marking tools.

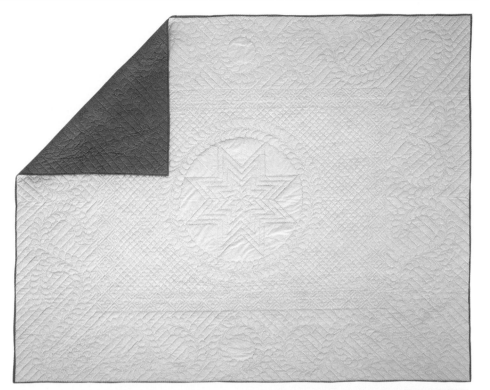

AMISH STAR. This whole-cloth is an all-quilted version of the classic circle-in-a-square Pennsylvania Amish quilt. It has a giant feather circle enclosing the center star, feather circles on the sides to make the quilt rectangular instead of square, and deep horseshoe-shaped corner scroll motifs, as well as a pumpkin seed inner border. Full instructions for making this quilt are in Chapter V. (Amish Star, 82″ x 94″, designed by Liz Porter, quilted by Barb Corsbie.)

Prepare Patterns

As you have learned by working through the exercises in this book, feather quilting designs must be drawn on paper before they can be transferred to cloth. If you wish to use any of the whole-cloth schemes given in this chapter, you must use large sheets of paper to create patterns of the design sections of the quilt before you can trace the designs on the fabric. Tracing paper, wide freezer paper or white butcher paper from the grocery store work well. Specific instructions for making the Princess Feather, True Lover's Knot, and Amish Star patterns are on following pages. In all cases, you only need to draw a fourth or a half of the central motif. The shading on the whole quilt diagrams indicates which elements must be drawn on paper. The Princess Feather requires two paper patterns for the inner quilt, a side border repeat, and end repeat and a corner, five elements in all. The True Lover's Knot calls for two paper patterns for the inner quilt (the knot and the heart), a border repeat that is used both on the sides and ends, and a corner motif, four elements in all. The Amish Star requires one quarter of the center star-ring, the border curls, the side circle and the corner, only four paper patterns in all, plus the Pumpkin Seed border motif.

When making these paper patterns, you don't need to draw in the individual feathers. You simply draw the center vein and outer guidelines. Then, when the paper patterns are placed under the quilt, you can trace on the center vein only, and make individual feather templates, as described in Chapter III, to mark the feathers. Illustrations showing what each paper pattern should look like for the Princess Feather, Amish Star and True Lover's Knot are included on their instruction pages.

If you are designing your own whole-cloth, start with a rough scale drawing similar to the drawings given for the quilts in this chapter, so you can get an idea how big your paper patterns should be. Use the skills you learned in Chapters I and II to work your ideas out on large paper. Lay the drawings under the cloth (prepared as described below) to see if the design you want will work. Refine the design elements as needed until you are satisfied with them.

Once your paper patterns are completed, you are ready to prepare your fabric for marking.

Figure 1

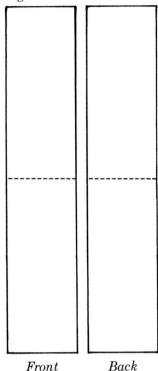

*Front
6 yards*   *Back
6 yards*

Figure 2

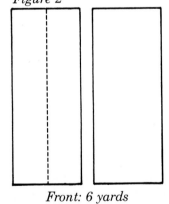

Front: 6 yards

Figure 3

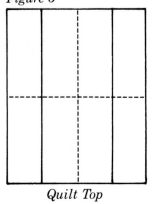

Quilt Top

Prepare the Top for Marking

1. Tear or cut each of the two 6 yard lengths of fabric in half, so that you have two 3 yard pieces for the front and two 3 yard pieces for the back of the quilt (Figure 1). For the purpose of these instructions, the **front** of the quilt refers to the lighter of the two fabrics. This is the side that will be marked, and the side you will quilt from, even though you can eventually use the quilt with either side up.
2. Prewash the fabric pieces. I use warm water, large load, no detergent. Line or tumble dry. Don't use fabric softener.
3. Tear or cut one of the pieces for the front and one of the pieces for the back down the middle lengthwise (Figure 2). Press all the panels.
4. For each side of the quilt, sew the two narrow panels to opposite sides of the wide panel. Be sure to keep the lengthwise grain lines going the same direction on all three panels. Even a piece of muslin flipped end to end can change color slightly, just as corduroy does more noticeably. Match the selvages and machine stitch, taking ½″ seam. Trim off the selvages, leaving a ¼″ seam. Press the seams for the front of the quilt **away** from the center. Press the seams for the back of the quilt **toward** the center. Set the backing fabric aside.
5. Fold the prepared quilt top in half lengthwise and press a lengthwise center guideline. Without unfolding, fold the quilt in half the other way and press a crosswise center guideline. When unfolded, your top will be creased into four equal quadrants (Figure 3).

Mark the Quilt Top

Chapter III gave instructions for marking individual feathers in continuous borders as you quilt. However, for a big feathering project like a whole-cloth quilt, all the marking should be done preliminary to basting and quilting.

1. Lay the 36″ x 60″ cardboard grid-ruled cutting board on a table. If you don't have a big table at home, work at a church or meeting hall that has two banquet-type tables you can put together to work on.
2. Lay your prepared fabric over the ruled cardboard, so that one of the four quadrants of the top is covering the board. Have the exact center of the quilt top at one corner of the grid ("x" in Figure 4). Align lengthwise and crosswise crease lines with the outer grid lines on the board. Pin the cloth into the cutting board.
3. Using your ruler, section off the quilt top by tracing lines that are darkened on the whole quilt diagram on the design area. Dividing up the quilt top into major design areas gets it under control for you. **Since not all of these sectioning lines will be quilted, you must make marks that are removable.**
4. Place the paper patterns under the various sections of the top and mark on center veins and other quilting lines. Make an individual feather template to use for the actual feathering. Use the feather template to mark feather scallops on both sides of the center vein, spacing the tails as needed to feather the hills and valleys, flipping the template over to do one side or the other, so that you have right sides of hearts on one side of the vein and left sides of hearts on the other. You may need two or three sizes of individual feather templates since feathers are wider in some parts of the designs than others. Patterns for several useful sizes of individual feather templates are in the **Treasury** appendix. Use the patterns and templates to mark the feather and other motifs on the entire quilt top.

Adding Grids

The Princess Feather has a 1" grid, diagonally set, in the inner oval, and a 2" grid in the middle area. The True Lover's Knot has a 2" grid over most of the quilt, with a ½" grid within the loops of the knot and inside the four hearts. The Amish Star has a 1" diagonal grid in the center section and parallel lines in the border areas. Marking such grids on cloth is really tricky because of fabric's tendency to stretch and shift as it is moved. The best way I have found to mark grids is with the cardboard sewing board described above and used to section off the quilt top. Lay the quilt top over the board, straight with the grid if you want a square grid, diagonally if you want a diagonal one. Using a ruler, trace the grid lines onto the cloth. Shift the quilt top around gently to get the grid on the sections where you want it. Poke pins through the quilt top into the cutting board to hold the fabric in place.

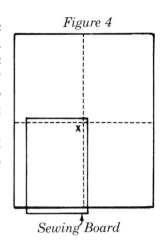

Figure 4

Sewing Board

Basting the Quilt

Once your quilt top is completely marked, you are ready to layer and baste it for quilting. Here again, this job can be made easy if you have access to two long banquet-style tables. A friend to help is another real advantage.

Gently press vertical and horizontal guidelines in the quilt backing. Lay the backing, seams side up, on the basting tables. Align the lengthwise crease with the crack between the two tables. Fold the batting in half lengthwise and lay it on half the backing, aligning the fold of the batting with the lengthwise crease of the backing. Open out the batting and smooth out any bumps. (Some quilters recommend opening the package and unfolding the batting the day before basting and letting the batt "relax" overnight.)

Fold the marked top in half lengthwise, right sides together, and lay it on half the batting, aligning the fold with the table crack. Open out the marked quilt top.

Do the first basting along the two seams of the fabric, aligning them perfectly as you baste. If your top and bottom fabrics are not the same width, just be sure the top fabric is perfectly centered over the bottom one. Baste the seams, and then baste the entire quilt, basting from the center out, or in a grid fashion, but, in either case, having basting about 6" apart.

Quilting

Whether you quilt with a hoop as I do, or with the quilt rolled in a frame, quilt any piece from the center out. See page 42 on how to quilt feathers.

Binding

If you want a scalloped binding like the one on the Princess Feather (Page 25) and the True Lover's Knot, (Page 21) measure out an equal distance (about 2") from the outer lines of quilting all the way around. Make small marks and connect them to form a binding placement line. Use a single fold bias binding cut about 1½" wide.

Lay a raw edge of binding on the marked line and machine stitch, using the presser foot as a guide. Once the binding is sewn on, trim excess top, batting and backing. Turn binding to other side and hand finish. Straight edges like on the Amish Star may also require measuring and marking in order to create a placement line for binding. A wider, French-fold binding works well for straight edges. Cut binding 2¼" wide, fold in half and press. Place raw edges of binding against placement line and machine stitch. Bring fold to other side and hand finish.

Note: In Chapter III you learned to customize various kinds of feather motifs. Designs like the central wheel of the Princess Feather and its corner scrolls, as well as the circles and corner designs of the Amish Star, fall into the "Circles and Other Shapes" category. For this type of motif, you were taught to start with all outer guidelines and work in from there to establish a center guideline. The designs for the Princess Feather, True Lover's Knot and Amish Star quilts were originated in that fashion. However, the instructions that follow for making paper patterns for these designs will usually have you start with the center vein. Don't be confused by this seeming change in procedure. It only occurs because the customizing steps for the designs in these quilts have already been taken for you.

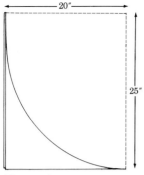

Figure 1

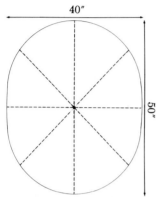

Figure 2

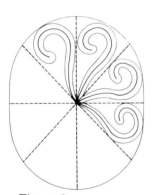

Figure 3

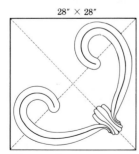

Figure 4

Princess Feather (78″ x 98″), designed by Marianne Fons

1. To make the center oval, fold a 40″ x 50″ paper rectangle in fourths. (You may have to tape two pieces of paper together to get this size.) Draw one fourth of the oval shape on one quadrant of the paper and cut on the drawn line (Figure 1).

2. Open out the oval. Darken horizontal and vertical crease lines. Fold the oval diagonally both ways to make more guiding creases (Figure 2). You need not darken the diagonal folds.

3. Notice the shaded four-plume area on the diagram, half of the Princess Feather wheel. With a pencil, draw in the four plumes, two short and two long. Remember how, in Chapter II, you learned to customize various types of feather designs. These Princess Feather plumes fall in the "other shapes" category (page 33). First sketch in the plume-shaped area that needs to be filled, forming an outer guideline. Then draw the center vein through the middle (Figure 3). A compass or household template can be used to help make the circular areas neat and accurate. Darken the center vein and thicken it to make a double vein. Also darken the outer guidelines so you will be able to see them through the cloth. Your paper pattern will look like Figure 3.

4. To make the corner scroll, use a piece of paper 28″ x 28″. Fold it in half diagonally both ways. Referring to the diagram below, draw one side of the scroll. You need the shell-shaped base part of the design, the center vein, and outer guidelines. Once you have drawn one side of the pattern, fold the paper back diagonally and trace the other half. With black marking pen, darken the shell design, center vein and outer guidelines. Your paper pattern will look like Figure 4.

5. The next patterns to make are the border repeats for the combination cable/feather border. Because the quilt is a rectangle, you'll need two different repeats, one for the side borders and one for the end borders. The repeat length for the sides is 16″. The repeat length for the end borders is 15″. Measure and cut two pieces of tracing paper, one for forming each repeat. Make the paper for the sides 8″ x 16″ and the paper for the ends 8″ x 15″. As you can see in the diagram, the width of the border area is actually 9″, but you must make the tracing paper 8″ wide in order to allow margin to each side of the quilting. Following instructions on page 19, fold and form the two repeats. Continue with the instructions on interwoven repeats (page 28). You need to draw only the center vein and outer guidelines for the plume part of the design. Carefully draw in the cable lines, using a ruler to make them an equal distance apart. Your repeats will look like Figures 5 and 6. After forming the two folded paper repeats, you can glue them to other pieces of paper the exact finished width of the border area (9″). This will make designing the corner easier and will make placing the pattern under the fabric easier.

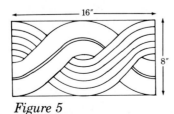

Figure 5

Figure 6

Figure 7

9"

15"

19"

28"

98"

9"

9"

8"

78"

*See Photo
on Page 25*

6. The remaining paper pattern to make is the corner design. Measure and cut a piece of paper 9" x 9". Sketch, fold and trace to form a center vein, outer guidelines and cable lines. Lay your side and end repeats next to the corner pattern to make sure the lines will connect satisfactorily. Your paper pattern will look like Figure 7.

7. Once you have made the five paper patterns, you can prepare your fabric for marking as described in Chapter III. Lay the various design element patterns under the quilt top fabric and

mark, using individual feathering templates as described on page 40. The 2" and 2½" patterns for individual templates given on Insert #4 will probably fit your patterns best. The cut edge of the paper oval serves as a guide for marking that shape on the fabric. To make a double oval, mark a second line on the fabric, ¼" out from the first one. After marking the feather motifs, continue following instructions on page 47 for adding grids, basting, quilting and binding.

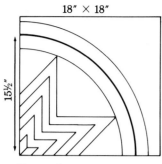

18″ × 18″

15½″

Figure 1

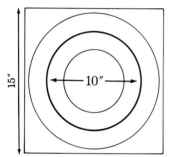

15″

10″

Figure 2

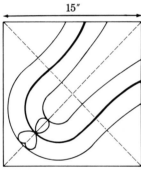

15″

Figure 3

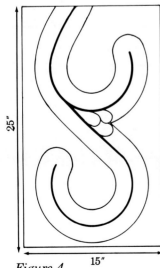

25″

15″

Figure 4

Amish Star (82″ x 94″), designed by Liz Porter

1. Measure and cut out a piece of paper 18″ x 18″. (You may have to tape two pieces of paper together to get this size.) One quarter of the eight-pointed star is printed on Insert #4. Lay your paper over the printed pattern, aligning a corner of the paper square with the center point of the star. Using a ruler to help you make straight lines, trace the quarter star on the paper.

2. The center vein of the circle is 15½″ away from the center point of the star (i.e., the center vein is a 31″ diameter circle). Improvise a big-circle compass by using a pencil tied to a length of string. Draw the circle. Darken the center vein and thicken it to make a double vein. Measure 2½″ out to each side of the center vein and sketch in outer guidelines for the large feather circle. Darken the outer guidelines so you will be able to see them through the cloth. Your paper pattern will look like Figure 1. You will use an individual feather template, as described on page 40, to feather the circle.

3. The center vein of the side border rings is a 10″ diameter circle. Use a piece of paper 15″ x 15″. Fold the square in half vertically and horizontally. Use a compass or household template to draw the 10″ center vein circle. Darken the center vein and thicken it to make a double vein. Measure out 2″ to each side of the center vein and draw outer guidelines for the feathers. Darken the outer guidelines. Your paper pattern will look like Figure 2.

4. To make the horseshoe-shaped corner motif, measure and cut another 15″ square of paper. Fold the square diagonally. Referring to the measurements on the quilt diagram, draw the center vein. Measure out 2″ from the center vein on each side and sketch in outer guidelines; darken the guidelines. Make a heart and teardrop at the base of the horseshoe as shown. Your paper pattern will look like Figure 3.

5. The remaining paper pattern to be made is for the double partial-circle plume for the borders. Use a piece of paper 15″ wide by 25″ long. Fold it lengthwise to make a center guideline. The center point of the circle closest to the corner is 6½″ from one short end of the paper. Use a compass or household template to draw a 9″ diameter circle that will be the center vein. The center of the circle closest to the midpoint of the side of the quilt is 12″ from the center point of the first circle you drew. Draw this 9″ diameter center vein circle as you did the previous one. Referring to the diagram, and Figure 4, connect the lines to form the center vein of the double partial-circle. Darken the center vein and thicken it to form a double center vein. Measure out 2″ from the center vein lines and sketch in outer guidelines. Your paper pattern will look like Figure 4. Darken outer guidelines so you will be able to see them through the cloth when adding the feathers.

6. Once you have made the four paper patterns for the Amish Star, you are ready to prepare your quilt top fabric for marking as described in Chapter III, sectioning off the main portions of the top as instructed. Lay the various design elements under the fabric and use individual feathering templates to mark on the feathers. Mark the Pumpkin Seed border as described next.

See Photo on Page 44

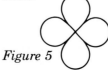

Figure 5

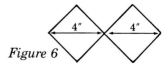

4″   4″

Figure 6

Pumpkin Seed Border

The double figure-eight motif (Figure 5) used for the narrow inner border of the Amish Star represents four pumpkin seeds placed together with their points touching. A full size pattern for the design is on insert #4 . It can be traced to make a paper pattern or a template for marking. The straight lines of the border should be marked first.

To mark the straight lines, first study the quilt diagram below. The pumpkin seed border is 4″ across (Figure 6). Figure 7 is a detail of the border, showing you where to begin marking. First make tiny marks 4″ apart on both sides of the border all the way around. Notice that the first marks are only 2″ from the corners. Connect the marks, forming the diagonally set boxes.

To mark the remaining straight lines, make two triangle templates with the dimensions given in Figure 8. First center the bigger triangle with its hypotenuse (long side) on the outer border line and mark along the template's right-angle edges (Figure 9). Then center the smaller template in the same fashion and mark its edges (Figure 10). Use a ruler to make the remaining straight lines at the corner. Add the pumpkin seed motif in each box.

After marking the feather motifs, continue following instructions on page 47 for adding grids, basting the quilt, quilting and binding.

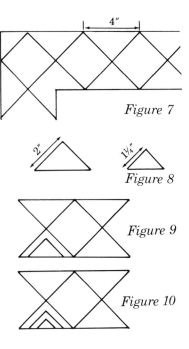

Figure 7

Figure 8

Figure 9

Figure 10

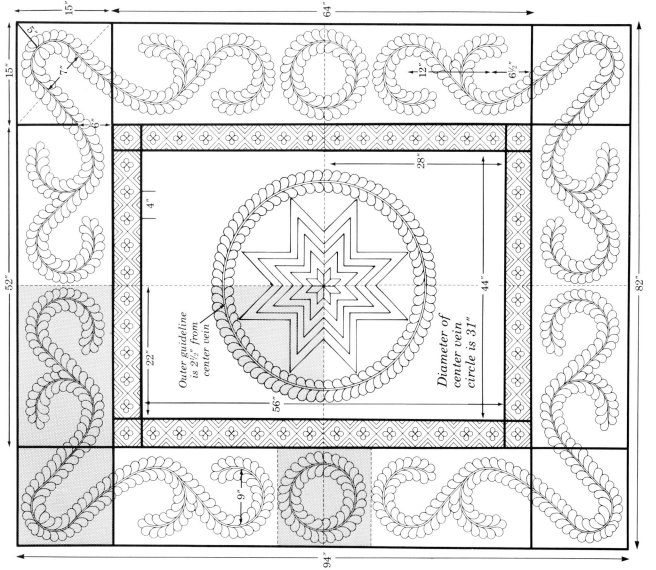

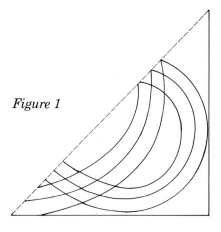

Figure 1

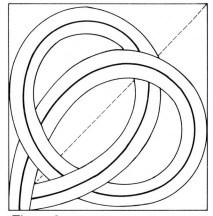

Figure 2

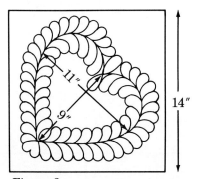

Figure 3

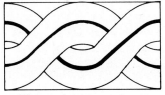

Figure 4

True Lover's Knot (80″ x 100″), designed by Liz Porter

1. To make the pattern for the loops of the central knot motif of the quilt, first measure and cut a piece of paper 19″ x 19″. Referring to the measurements on the quilt diagram and Figures 1 and 2, sketch in the outer guidelines of the loops and the center veins. First, fold the paper in half diagonally and draw in only one-half of the loops; flip the paper and trace the loops on the other diagonal half of the paper so the loops will be symmetrical. You will have to open out the square in order to properly position the "over" and "under" portions of the knot. The width of the feather loops is 3″. Use a wide-tipped permanent black marking pen to darken and thicken the center vein so it will be a double vein. Darken the outer guidelines too, so you will be able to see them through the cloth of your quilt top. Your paper pattern will look like Figure 2.

2. To make the feather heart pattern, use a piece of paper 14″ x 14″. Follow the instructions on page 15 to draw the feather heart. Refer to Figure 3 and quilt photograph on page 21 while drawing the heart.

3. The length of the border repeat is 20″ both for the side borders and the end borders of the quilt. The width of the border area, as indicated on the quilt diagram, is 10″. The width of the interwoven feather design is 8″, in order to allow margin to each side of the stitching. Measure and cut a piece of tracing paper 8″ x 20″. Following instructions on interwoven borders on page 28, fold the paper to form the repeat pattern. Your paper pattern will look like Figure 4 at left. After forming the double repeat, you can glue the tracing paper to a 10″ x 20″ piece of paper or cardboard. This will make designing the corner easier and make placing the pattern under the cloth simpler. Darken and thicken the center vein lines and darken the outer guidelines so you will be able to see them through your quilt top fabric.

4. Draw the corner on a 10″ x 10″ piece of paper. Refer to Figure 5 to form the interlaced loops. Your paper pattern will look like Figure 6.

5. Once you have made the four paper patterns, you can prepare your fabric for marking as described in Chapter III. Lay the various design element patterns under the quilt top fabric and mark, using individual feathering templates. The 1¾″ size feather template pattern (Insert #4) will fit the True Lover's Knot designs best. See page 47 regarding the addition of grid quilting lines.

See Photo on Page 21

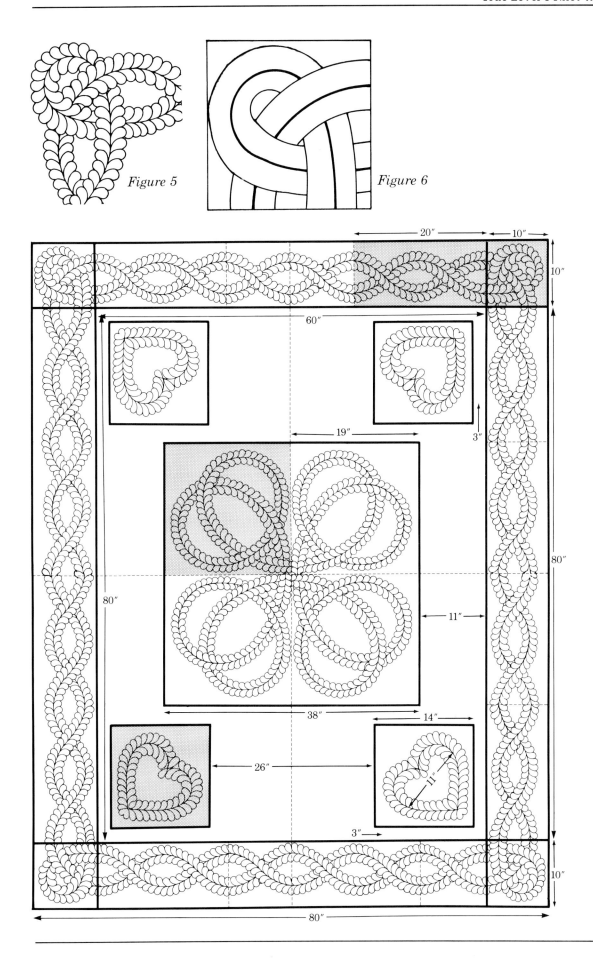

Figure 5

Figure 6

A Treasury of Feather Designs

The **Treasury** appears on pages 54 and 55, as well as on Inserts #3 and #4. Most of the quilting designs in this section were gleaned from photographs of antique quilts. Others were sketched at quilt shows. A few are variations I have devised through my own experimentation. The small drawings on circle options, border options and miscellaneous motifs can be made any size using the skills gained by working through Chapters I and II of this book. The large designs are presented with the idea that they might fit projects you have, but they can also be customized for any size quilting area. Small sketches on the full size design pages show how to combine or use them for specific size spaces.

If you already own books of full size feather quilting designs, don't feel that knowing how to create your own designs makes these books obsolete. In fact, they are more valuable to you than ever before, because now you know how to revise the designs within them to fit your projects perfectly.

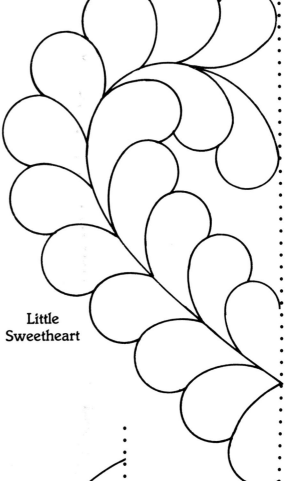

Little Sweetheart

Tulip Double Plume

Little Sweetheart fits a 6″ diagonal square

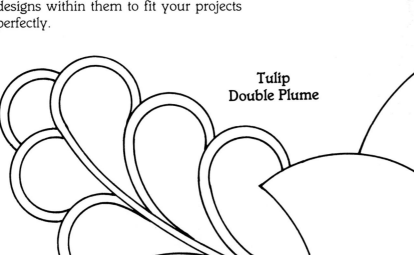

Repeat Tulip Plume for 6″ wide scalloped border

Circle
Options

Bibliography

American Patchwork Quilt (Exhibition Catalog). The Denver Art Museum, 1986.

Anthony, Catherine, and Libby Lehman. **Quiltmaker's Big Book of Pattern Grids.** Santa Clara, California: Leone Publications, 1983.

Binney, Edwin, 3rd, and Gail Binney-Winslow. **Homage to Amanda.** San Francisco: R K Press, 1984.

Bishop, Robert. **New Discoveries in American Quilts.** New York: E.P. Dutton & Company, Inc., 1975.

Bresenhan, Karoline Patterson, and Nancy O'Bryant Puentes. **Lone Stars, A Legacy of Texas Quilts, 1836-1936.** Austin: The University of Texas Press, 1986.

Colby, Averil. **Quilting.** New York: Charles Scribner's Sons, 1971.

Finley, John, and Jonathan Holstein. **Kentucky Quilts, 1800-1900.** Louisville: The Kentucky Quilt Project, Inc., 1982.

Fitzrandolph, Mavis. **Traditional Quilting.** London: B.T Batsford Ltd., 1954.

Fox, Sandi (Exhibition Supervisor). **19th Century American Patchwork Quilt (Exhibition Catalog).** Seibu Museum of Art, Japan.

Haders, Phyllis. **Sunshine and Shadow, The Amish and Their Quilts.** New York: Universe Books, 1976.

Haders, Phyllis. **The Warner Collector's Guide to American Quilts.** New York: Warner Books, Inc., 1981.

Hall, Carrie A., and Rose G. Kretsinger. **The Romance of the Patchwork Quilt in America.** New York: Bonanza Books, 1935.

Hoke, Donald (Compiler). **Dressing the Bed, Quilts and Coverlets from the Collections of the Milwaukee Public Museum.** Milwaukee: Milwaukee Public Museum, 1985.

Holstein, Jonathan. **The Pieced Quilt, an American Design Tradition.** Greenwich, Connecticut: New York Graphic Society, Ltd., 1973.

James, Michael. **The Quiltmaker's Handbook.** Englewood Cliffs, New Jersey: Prentice-Hall, Inc., 1978.

Johnson, Bruce, in collaboration with Susan S. Connor, Josephine Rogers and Holly Sidford. **A Child's Comfort, Baby and Doll Quilts in American Folk Art.** New York: Harcourt Brace Jovanovich in association with the Museum of American Folk Art, 1977.

Leone, Diana. **Fine Hand Quilting.** Los Altos, California: Leone Publications, 1986.

Nelson, Cyril I., and Carter Houck. **The Quilt Engagement Calendar Treasury.** New York: E.P. Dutton, Inc., 1982.

Orlofsky, Patsy, and Myron Orlofsky. **Quilts in America.** New York: McGraw-Hill, 1974.

Pottinger, David. **Quilts from the Indiana Amish.** New York: E.P. Dutton, Inc., 1983.

Safford, Carlton L., and Robert Bishop. **America's Quilts and Coverlets.** New York: E.P. Dutton, 1980.

Silber, Julie. **The Esprit Quilt Collection (Catalog).** San Francisco: Esprit De Corp, 1985.

Stitches in Time, A Legacy of Ozark Quilts, Rogers Historical Museum, Rogers, Arkansas, 1986.

Tomlonson, Judy Schroeder. **Mennonite Quilts and Pieces.** Intercourse, Pennsylvania: Good Books, 1985.

"To Quilt in the Name of Beauty" (No author listed). **Creative Ideas for Living Magazine,** July 1986, Birmingham, Alabama.

Townsend, Louise. "No Mark Quilting," **Quilter's Newsletter Magazine,** February, 1987, Wheatridge, Colorado.